ROBERT LATIMER

A STORY OF JUSTICE AND MERCY

ROBERT LATIMER

A STORY OF JUSTICE AND MERCY

GARY BAUSLAUGH

JAMES LORIMER & COMPANY LTD., PUBLISHERS
TORONTO

James Lorimer & Company Ltd., Publishers acknowledges the support of the Ontario Arts Council. We acknowledge the financial support of the Government of Canada through the Canada Book Fund for our publishing activities. We acknowledge the support of the Canada Council for the Arts for our publishing program. We acknowledge the Government of Ontario through the Ontario Media Development Corporation's Ontario Book Initiative.

Canada Council
for the Arts

Conseil des Arts
du Canada

Cover design: Meghan Collins

Library and Archives Canada Cataloguing in Publication

Bauslaugh, Gary
Robert Latimer: a story of justice and mercy / by Gary Bauslaugh.

Includes bibliographical references and index.
Issued also in electronic format.
ISBN 978-1-55277-519-6

1. Latimer, Robert W. (Robert William). 2. Latimer, Tracy, 1980-1993.
3. Trials (Euthanasia)--Canada. 4. Euthanasia--Moral and ethical aspects.
5. Euthanasia--Law and legislation--Canada. I. Title.

R726.B34 2010   179.7   C2010-902610-1

James Lorimer & Company Ltd., Publishers
317 Adelaide Street West, Suite 1002
Toronto, ON
M5V 1P9
www.lorimer.ca

Printed and bound in Hong Kong

CONTENTS

We can often get away with evil acts, but a good one will haunt us forever.

– Attributed to Gilbert Ryle

We hand folks over to God's mercy, and show none ourselves.

– George Eliot in *Adam Bede*

INTRODUCTION

Blessed are the merciful, for they shall obtain mercy.
—Matthew 5:7 (King James Version)

One reading of this famous passage from the Bible is that by being merciful we shall receive God's blessing and mercy in an afterlife. But the passage, in its beautiful simplicity and sentiment, has a different but equally compelling meaning for secularists.

The merciful are blessed, in a secular sense, because they enrich human life both in the way their acts of kindness help others and in the way they show us the better side of humanity. Although the merciful do not always obtain mercy directly, as this book will illustrate, they do show us the possibility of a kinder and more compassionate world.

Mercy evokes powerful human feelings. One of the most compelling scenes in theatre—the audience always gasps at this point in stage productions—occurs when the Bishop in *Les Misérables* encounters the officer who has apprehended Jean Valjean with silverware stolen from the Bishop, after the Bishop had taken in this poor man and trusted him. The Bishop, rather than denouncing the ungrateful thief, tells the officer that he gave Valjean the silverware, then adds some silver candlesticks to the gift.

In *The Merchant of Venice*, Portia's moving speech on the quality of mercy is one of the most quoted in all of Shakespeare:

The quality of mercy is not strain'd
It droppeth as the gentle rain from heaven
Upon the place beneath: It is twice bless'd;
It blesseth him that gives and him that takes…

We share a human desire to live in a world marked by kindness and compassion, even though our actual world so often seems otherwise. Perhaps that is why we treasure particular moments of human kindness; they remind us of how we would like to be, and how we would like the world to be.

Ending the life of another human usually represents the opposite of the kindness and compassion we value so highly. Most such actions are correctly called murder; they are committed with malice, and they are reprehensible. But on occasion the ending of a human life is done not out of malice, but out of love and mercy. These cases are the opposite of those that are malicious; they represent courageous acts of human love and kindness. Such acts of mercy are not murder.

For various reasons, some of which will be discussed in this book, our legal system in Canada fails to provide sufficient opportunity to make the critical distinction between selfless acts of mercy and cruel acts of murder. The one serves the interest of a dying person; the other is directly contrary to the interests of a living person. One serves to make a more compassionate society; the other the opposite. In a truly just society, we would try very hard not to conflate these two actions, which arise out of completely opposite motivations.

In Canada, do we try very hard to make the critical distinction between murder and euthanasia? And do we have effective mechanisms for making this distinction? In 1993, Robert Latimer, a Saskatchewan farmer, ended the life of his desperately ill daughter and for the following seventeen years has been entangled in legal proceedings that included seven years of imprisonment. Convicted of second-degree murder, he will be on parole for life.

There is no perfect system of justice, and there never will be. But justice systems must always seek justice; that is their purpose. Laws, and the administration of laws, must therefore be continually monitored and modified as legally sanctioned injustices become evident. The legal profession is fond of saying that "hard cases make bad laws," implying that we can't build a legal system on unusual and difficult cases. But it is at least as true to say that bad laws make hard cases. We cannot skew the legal system to account for highly unusual cases, but equally we cannot back away from changing laws when they are evidently unjust. And if existing laws lead to injustice, those administering the laws ought to seek ways of mitigating the impact of those laws. Acts of mercy are not acts of murder, whatever the laws happen to say. Bad laws, and strict adherence to those laws, make hard cases because they trap law enforcement officials into taking actions that are manifestly unfair.

The prosecution of Robert Latimer was a hard case because it was widely understood that he was not a criminal; that is, he did not act with criminal intent. Even those involved in his prosecution at times acknowledged this: the Crown Prosecutor in Latimer's second trial case said, in his summation, that Latimer had been "motivated by love, and I don't dispute that for a second." It is a bad law that leads to punishing an act of love with the same severity as we punish a malicious act of murder.

In this book, I discuss the Latimer case from the particular vantage point I have had in knowing the man and talking to him extensively over the past five years; from discussions with many of the people involved in his case, including his defence lawyer; from transcripts of various proceedings; from attending his momentous parole hearing in 2007; and from subsequent involvement in the consequences of that hearing. I also reflect on the ways that such cases illustrate both certain threats to our civil liberties, in the application of existing laws, and the need for new, more humane laws.

Do the merciful obtain mercy? I will let you be the judge.

CHAPTER 1
THE LATIMERS

Wilkie is one of hundreds of small rural Saskatchewan towns, most of them established along the train lines that gave market access to the vast wheat fields of that province. About 160 kilometres northwest of Saskatoon, the Wilkie townsite was first populated in the early 1900s as a stop along the new CPR line, which arrived in 1908. The town was incorporated in 1911 and named, for some reason, after the president of the Imperial Bank of Canada. Maybe that was to make it easier for the growing community to get loans.

The first grain elevator in Wilkie was built around the same time; elevators were being built frequently along the rail lines that were appearing all through the grain-growing areas, so farmers would have relatively short distances to travel by horse and wagon to get their crops on the way to markets. The picturesque elevators, which became a symbol of the province, are quickly disappearing now as modern trucking techniques allow for more centralized grain storage. Some towns would like to keep the old elevators, for aesthetic and historical reasons, but kids sneak into them and climb the towers, and many towns are arriving at the conclusion that it is just too dangerous to keep them standing.

Things are changing in rural Saskatchewan. Farms continue to get bigger as equipment has become too expensive for small farms, and economies of scale inexorably push against the viability of smaller family-run farms. Wilkie maintains an optimistic public face, though. In the spring of 2010

Wilkie's website proclaimed:

> *Tree-lined streets and friendly faces welcome you to Wilkie.*
> *As a prairie community, Wilkie radiates the warmth [that]*
> *epitomizes rural Saskatchewan.*
> *Meeting the medical and educational needs of all ages, Wilkie*
> *provides a safe and healthy family environment. Boasting a*
> *skilled labour force and a quality of life unequaled anywhere.*

The motto on the town's website is "A Pioneer Town that Keeps on Growing," despite the fact that the population, which was 1,500 in 1912, now stands at about 1,300. By all accounts, though, Wilkie is a warm and friendly community that, if not quite meeting all the medical and educational needs of all ages and if not exactly, by most reckonings, providing an unequalled quality of life, is undoubtedly a good place to live, with good people who look out for one another.

Robert Latimer is one of those good people. While he lived on a farm just outside Wilkie he had a reputation as a kind and honest man and a good, caring, hardworking husband and father. The Latimer farm, which Robert took over in 1978 from his parents Bill and Mae, covers about 518 hectacres. Located on Highway 29 about sixteen kilometres north of Wilkie, it is a "small" farm in a land of huge agribusinesses. Like many of their neighbours, the Latimers grow wheat and canola.

Bill bought the farm in 1948. It included some outbuildings and a somewhat dilapidated and not-well-insulated farmhouse that the family lived in during the summer. In the winter they moved into a more comfortable place in town. Marjorie, one of Robert's older sisters, says that staying at the old farmhouse was like camping out—rustic and fun. They all have good memories of those times. The original owner had planted a lot of trees on the property, and the children loved to play around the secluded grassy places hidden among the trees. Some years later Bill built a new house on the farm, and then lived there until Robert and Laura took the farm over and moved in. At that point, Bill and Mae moved into town.

Mae was married twice. Her first husband was Ralph Donald, and they had three children—Dale, then Marjorie or "Marj," and Barbara. In the

winter of 1942, Ralph came down with a serious tooth infection, something we do not now think of as a life-threatening ailment. But Ralph's
timing was bad. In mid-1942 there was only enough penicillin in the
United States to treat about ten patients. And Ralph was in snow-covered
northern Saskatchewan. His parents were able to get him to a doctor, but
his condition worsened and there was little the doctor could do. Ralph
died, leaving Mae with the three children, aged two, four, and six. Marj
can remember her father, but she does not know now how many of these
memories are real ones and how many come from pictures she has seen
and stories she has heard. Mae and the children had a hard time of it for a
while, but she was able to earn some money by teaching at a small school
in the Saskatchewan hamlet of Cloan, where she had been born. Then she
married Bill Latimer in 1947, and they bought the farm a year later. The
Latimers had four children: Pat, John, Robert, and Dorothy. There were
nineteen years between Mae's first child, Dale, and her youngest, Dorothy.
As of 2010, all her children are still alive.

Both Bill and Mae were raised in Saskatchewan. Bill was a good farmer
and a good provider, and when he and Mae got married, he took on his
three new children, as Marj says, "as though they were his own." Mae
always said she was lucky to have had "two good husbands."

Robert Latimer was born on March 13, 1953. His half-sister Marj was
sixteen years older than he was, and she remembers helping "with general baby care with Bob." Marj left home when Robert was still young,
but always kept in close touch. Marj says, "Bob was a high-spirited little
boy, but he was always kind. I don't ever remember him hurting anyone."
For a farm boy he was unusually sensitive in regard to what his younger
sister Dorothy, who later became a nurse, refers to as "blood and guts."
Dorothy remembers him fainting once in school, in Grade 8 or 9, after
getting an immunization shot. He especially hated going to the dentist.
Dorothy and the other children still at home liked to tease young Robert
about his squeamishness.

Robert, as he began to grow up, was not exactly a shy and retiring youth;
he went to lots of parties, did lots of drinking, and smoked some marijuana.
He ran into trouble with the law a few times then and received a conviction
for impaired driving in 1976. Two years before that, he and a friend were

convicted of sexual assault, but that conviction was overturned on appeal, on the grounds that there had been undue judicial pressure on the jury. The prosecutor declined to retry the case. This particular event has often been raised by those who want to suggest that there is something sinister about Latimer, but the episode was many years ago, he was only twenty-one, and the evidence about what happened was questionable.

After his youthful escapades in Wilkie, Robert spent some time in British Columbia as a young man. He worked in various places, including the Victoria shipyards. He obtained a pilot's licence at one point and remembers the thrill of flying over the beautiful Gulf Islands. He returned to Wilkie in 1977 and met Laura, who was visiting her grandmother there. Born in British Columbia, Laura was an attractive, capable, and smart young woman who was teaching in Kitimat. The young Latimer was strong and ruggedly handsome—later in life he began to look a bit like the Canadian actor Graham Greene—and he was maturing into a friendly, soft-spoken, and kind man. The two young people fell in love and got married in Kitimat in 1978. Then they settled down in Wilkie to run the family farm.

Robert was well liked and respected by his neighbours. One of them, Wilson Barker, has said that he was proud to have known Robert since the day he was born. He described his neighbour as "very strong, both physically and mentally. He had faith in himself." Robert worked hard on the land, getting help at harvest time. Another neighbour, who helped with some harvests in the early nineties, remarked that Robert was sometimes "grouchy," but that neither Robert nor Laura ever complained about anything.

Today, the family farm has about four hectares of yard around the modest three-bedroom frame bungalow that Bill and Mae built. Many of the original trees have been cut down, so it is more open than it was in the early days when Marj and the other children played there, but Robert has planted new trees that are starting to fill in now. There are a number of outbuildings, including two Quonset huts, a couple of sheds, a shop, and a very large hip-roofed barn. The barn was once used for cattle but now is used mostly for storing machinery. Robert, on the farm, is almost obsessively tidy—something that his brothers and sisters frequently tease him about.

Both Robert and Laura are well liked and respected in the community.

They are members of the Wilkie United Church, which Laura still attends. Their children are Tracy, born in 1980; Brian, born in 1983; Lindsay, their second daughter, born in 1985; and Lee, their second son, born in August, 1993, two months before Tracy died.

※

Tracy Lynn Latimer was born on November 23, 1980, in the small hospital in North Battleford, Saskatchewan, about a half-hour drive from the Latimer farm. After an "uneventful" pregnancy, Laura and Robert arrived at the hospital around nine a.m. on the twenty-second, and the birth took place about twenty-four hours later.

But the birthing process was not so uneventful. At some point Tracy suffered severe brain damage as a result of oxygen deprivation. The Latimers never found out exactly what happened because the hospital, likely fearing a lawsuit, was cagey about what information it would release to them. The Latimers could have found out more by launching a suit, but it was not in their nature to do so. But Robert said later that they would never go back to that hospital again for any future births.

What the Latimers did know was that during Laura's long labour she had bled the whole time. Because the fetal heart monitor was broken it couldn't be used to monitor the baby's heart rate, which was mistakenly thought to be much higher than it was. Once the actual rate was discovered, the doctor made a decision to extract the baby immediately, using forceps. Laura said that Tracy looked dead when she first saw her: "…usually a baby will have their knees drawn up to their tummy, but she was flat, just literally flat… And they started to work on her right away, they got her breathing, they wheeled her by me…I wasn't to hold her or anything, but they did allow me to see her for a minute, and then they took her away."

Robert noticed signs of unusual behaviour almost immediately. The baby's fingers were twitching. He asked a nurse about it, and she incorrectly said it was due to hypoglycemia, a fairly common condition in newborns.

At four the next morning Laura was wakened by a doctor and a nurse. They told her that the baby was having seizures and that she would have to be taken immediately to the Royal University Hospital in Saskatoon, about 145 kilometres away. Tracy was taken in an incubator, by ambulance, with the Latimers following by car.

After arriving at University Hospital, Tracy was put into a drug-induced coma for about eight days, to lessen the swelling in her brain and to lessen the seizure activity. Finally, after five days, Laura was allowed to hold her baby, though Tracy was comatose. When Tracy was awakened the seizures seemed to have been stopped, probably with the aid of phenobarbital. By this time the medical staff knew that Tracy had brain damage, but they did not know how much. That would be determined by observations over Tracy's first year. Everyone hoped it would not be too severe.

Tracy had no seizures when she got home—a good sign—and she was taken off the medication. Laura described her as a "happy little baby." But at four or five months Laura and Robert noticed her hand twitching again, pretty well continuously—not a good sign. They took Tracy to a doctor in North Battleford, who believed the twitching was from seizures. Fearing the constant seizures could further damage the little girl's brain, he made an appointment for Tracy to see a neurologist at University Hospital in six weeks' time. The Latimer family went home to wait, but Bob and Laura could not bear the idea of biding their time for so long, especially since the seizures might be causing more brain damage. They contacted the hospital themselves and were told to bring Tracy in right away. Tracy was admitted immediately and remained for three weeks. The doctors tried different drugs to control the seizures, but when they sent her home she was still twitching continuously, at least while she was awake.

During the first four years of Tracy's life, the Latimers worked with doctors at University Hospital to determine which medications would best control her seizures. She was eventually given the drug clonazepam (brand name Rivotril) in combination with another drug, Tegretol, which reduced the seizures to five or six a day. That was the number of seizures Tracy continued to have every day for the rest of her life. The doctors told the Latimers that during those initial months, when the seizures were uncontrolled, Tracy likely suffered additional brain damage.

The drugs to suppress the involuntary movements of the seizures also induced lethargy and exacerbated the damage that had already been done to such vital functions as breathing and digestion. During her first few years Tracy could not swallow food, which had to be massaged down her throat. She vomited frequently and continued to have problems breathing.

Although unable to move like normal babies, she could, when she was small, roll across the room. But, as Laura said, "She didn't purposefully reach over and pick up something and bring it to her mouth or anything like that." That simple action of a baby's putting an object in its mouth, something that causes anxious moments for parents of normal children, would have brought joy to the Latimers. But it never happened.

Tracy's difficult start was the beginning of a difficult life. Tracy's condition is known as cerebral palsy, the medical definition of which is, "a non-progressive but not unchanging disorder of movement and/or posture, due to an insult to or anomaly of the developing brain." "Non-progressive" means that it is due to a one-time event that causes permanent damage, but it is "not unchanging" because the effects of the damage can cause increasing bodily damage, especially in severe cases. Some sort of trauma to the brain, usually oxygen deprivation, interferes with the brain's ability to communicate with the body, usually causing involuntary body movements. Some cases of cerebral palsy, about a sixth of them, are relatively benign, sometimes noticeable only as a slight physical awkwardness. Only about a third of the cases are quite severe, and only a small proportion of those are as severe as Tracy's. Most people with cerebral palsy lead relatively normal lives; these people, the majority, are not mentally compromised and they have normal lifespans.

Not so with Tracy. Dr. Anne Dzus, an orthopaedic surgeon who first examined Tracy in 1985, described her as having "one of the worst forms of cerebral palsy in that she was totally body-involved. Her total body was involved from her head right down to her toes so all four limbs, her brain, her back, everything was involved..." Such severe cases often result in cognitive problems as well. In Tracy's case, she was locked into the mental capacity of a four- or five-month-old baby.

Tracy's first operation, when she was four years old, was to ease muscle tension in her left leg; but the result was increased pain through involuntary movements in her right leg. And Tracy could no longer roll over and bat at toys as she used to do. Pain was starting to become a factor in her life, but nothing stronger than Tylenol could be given to her because stronger medications would further suppress muscle reflexes that were already suppressed by her anti-seizure drugs. This would have made her essentially comatose, requiring hospitalization for life support.

Laura and Robert worked hard to cope with the challenge of raising a severely compromised child. Laura said it was like having a little baby "you have to do everything for," except that in Tracy's case it would continue for her entire life. Still, Laura and Robert loved her; she was their daughter. And she brought them closer together. Laura said that "If one got depressed, the other person would be up and say, we'll get through this...Tracy will get through, we'll be all right." But Laura cried herself to sleep for a year, grieving over what had happened to her baby. After that she just decided to stop the crying and accept the way things were.

After a few years, when Tracy was seven, one of the anti-seizure drugs she was taking, Tegretol, was determined to have reached a toxic level in her system. Robert explains, "The Tegretol problem left Tracy vomiting for four to six months, stuff the consistency of coffee grounds. Tracy would be fed, and the food would be thrown up. So milk would be given to her, and some food she could keep down at times. But it was hard to feed her enough food without her throwing up, so often by evening she would be dehydrated, and we would take her to the Wilkie hospital, and a doctor would give her liquid intravenously. Before it was determined that Tegretol was the problem, a doctor from Saskatoon was recommending that Tracy have a feeding tube cut into her stomach. We were told Tegretol is a drug that is hard to gauge its level of toxicity and that was the reason for it taking so long to decide to stop giving it to Tracy. She continued on with only one drug, clonazepam, to control her seizures the rest of her life, and her stomach problems improved."

Because the cerebral palsy affected Tracy's entire body she eventually developed scoliosis, an abnormal curvature and rotation of the back. Tracy, like most children with this severe form of cerebral palsy, started to develop partially dislocated hip joints because of muscle imbalance and abnormal signals from the brain. The hip problem became a source of considerable pain, which lasted for the rest of her life.

By March 1989, when Tracy was eight, the scoliosis had progressed to the point where her backbone was fifty degrees out of alignment, which Dr. Dzus considered to be very significant. Vital organs were now being compressed by the spinal curvature, and Tracy continued to suffer convulsions and vomiting. Furthermore, the tendency of Tracy's hip to dislocate was becoming a real problem. To ease the situation, Dr. Dzus operated in February of 1990, trying to balance the various muscle pressures by lengthening some muscle tissues and cutting some tendons. Tracy emerged in a much more symmetrical condition. Although her scoliosis was still active, she seemed better off than she had been.

Tracy had another examination by Dr. Dzus in March 1992, when she was eleven years old. Her hip was becoming more problematic and her spinal curvature was now sixty-seven degrees. Left untreated, Tracy's rib cage would likely begin to press on her pelvis, possibly causing a lot of pain and perhaps even death. Another surgery was carried out on August 27, 1992. By this time the curvature was seventy-three degrees. Dr. Dzus was able to get it back to about fifteen degrees by putting L-shaped stainless steel rods on either side of Tracy's spine, with wires to hold them in position. The lower ends of the Ls went though holes drilled in her pelvis. Dr. Dzus described this as "major surgery," taking seven to eight hours, but the sort of thing often needed by children with medical conditions as severe as Tracy's.

Although complications from such surgery often occur, Tracy had none of significance. Dr. Dzus said that she "came through it very, very well." She saw Tracy again on September 16 and noted again that she was doing quite well, no longer vomiting as she had after the operation and sleeping better. Her wound had healed and, with the aid of the rods in her back, she was able to sit up more comfortably. Her hips did not seem too bad, according to Dr. Dzus, although her right hip—the one that had always been the most problematic—looked as though it could cause trouble. Dr. Dzus saw Tracy again on November fourth, and again Tracy seemed to be improving. In particular, she was able to sit for long periods of time, something that is very difficult for children with untreated scoliosis. Nevertheless, her right hip was now causing her considerable pain. Dr. Dzus thought that an operation would be necessary on the hip, and she discussed this with the Latimers, but wanted to wait until Tracy had more fully recovered from the trauma of the back surgery.

Throughout all of these discussions and procedures, the Latimers remained worried. Although the uncramping of Tracy's lungs and stomach had improved her breathing and eating, the rods made her body stiff. "She was rigid as a board," Laura observed. "Before the surgery she was flexible. You could sit and rock with her, and she loved to be rocked...Bob used to rock her for hours..." But now most positions were uncomfortable for her, and sleeping was more of a problem. And so was the hip. "Tracy was never the same again [after the operation], never. She was never the happy person she used to be, ever, ever again. She couldn't cuddle any more, she couldn't rock..."

The prospects for Tracy were not good. Even Dr. Dzus, who was focused on trying to improve Tracy's life, had trouble being optimistic. She noted that Tracy could sit and breathe more easily after the surgery and no longer vomited as much, but admitted she was suffering in other ways. Tracy had lost her flexibility and was in severe pain, most likely because of her hip.

To Tracy's parents, the picture seemed even grimmer. Dr. Dzus was looking at what she could do that might help. The Latimers were watching their daughter suffer and fearing the increasing deterioration of her compromised body, whatever Dr. Dzus might do.

The next visit to Dr. Dzus was in February 1993. Tracy was suffering from her right hip, which by now was dislocated. Dr. Dzus told the Latimers that she thought it was still too soon for more corrective surgery, so she scheduled another appointment for the fall.

Laura gave birth to the Latimers' fourth child, Lee, on August 11. Having Tracy at home during the final months of her pregnancy was too much for Laura to manage, so from July 5 to October 1 Tracy was cared for at a North Battleford group home. Staff at the home reported that Tracy did quite well while she was there, although they noted that she had some pain and lost some weight. In fact, Tracy lost about one-sixth of her body weight while she was there and was down to about thirty-eight pounds. She ate well only when her mother was helping her. The Latimers also found that by this time she was not sleeping well, probably because of the pain from her hip.

The final appointment with Dr. Dzus—the fateful one—was on October 12, 1993.

Laura and Tracy went to that last appointment on their own, without Robert, who was very busy with harvesting. The main thing Dr. Dzus remembered from that meeting was Tracy's extreme pain: "She was lying on the examining table when I came in," Dr. Dzus testified. "Her mother was holding her right leg in a fixed flexed position with her knee in the air and any time you tried to move that leg Tracy expressed pain, and her way of expressing pain was to cry out." While her left hip seemed all right and her surgically repaired back seemed fine, her right hip could not be moved without causing severe pain.

Some sort of surgery was needed to reduce her distress, and Dr. Dzus discussed the options with Laura. Major hip reconstruction—reassembling the ball and socket—would be feasible only if the cartilage on the joint were healthy enough for it to be put back inside the socket along with the ball of the femur, which also could not be too damaged. X-rays showed that this probably would not work for Tracy; the ball joint was too badly eroded, and the cartilage was probably too badly worn. The only real recourse then would be, as Dr. Dzus put it, "a salvage job." She explained that this meant removing parts of the ball and socket, covering the head of the femur with tissue, and leaving it unconnected as a "flail joint." This is a general term for any joint that has an excessive amount of mobility. In Tracy's case there would be no bone connection at all, just a space that would eventually fill up with scar tissue. Dr. Dzus anticipated that the top quarter of her femur would have to be cut off and removed. This operation, called "resection arthroplasty," is sometimes done instead of a hip replacement. Those who have this operation are usually relieved of pain, eventually, but have difficulty walking because of problems in controlling the movement of the resulting flail joint. But then, Tracy never had been able to walk, and never would be able to do so.

Dr. Dzus's news came as a shock to Laura. "I was stunned," she said later. "I was absolutely stunned. I couldn't stop crying." Dr. Dzus had been talking for years about the eventual need for hip surgery, but she had always described it in terms of a reconstructive procedure. This was the first time she had suggested that the hip might be too far gone for that.

And the outlook, even with surgery, was not good. Dr. Dzus observed that, although the spinal rods had helped Tracy in some ways, the lack of mobility the rods caused was creating other problems. Because she was moving less, she was developing bed sores. Her weight loss and her pain all contributed to a deteriorating quality of life. Even if this proposed surgery was successful, Tracy would probably need more surgical interventions in the future. It seemed likely she would need surgery on her left hip and to have a feeding tube inserted into her stomach to bypass the mouth and swallowing mechanism. Clearly, given her weight loss, nutrition was becoming a major problem.

Even more upsetting to Laura was that, as Dr. Druz explained, "the postoperative pain can be incredible." It can be mitigated in hospital, for a time, by using epidural catheters to freeze the bottom half of the body, but eventually the child has to leave the hospital. Recovery would take "a good year, and maybe even longer."

Because of the severity of Tracy's pain, Dr. Dzus wanted to schedule the surgery as soon as possible. She happened to have a cancellation on November 4, 1993, and scheduled the operation for then. Tracy was to be brought in a day earlier so that her weight loss could be investigated. If blood tests indicated she might not survive the operation, the surgery would be temporarily cancelled until they could get Tracy into "optimum shape," as Dr. Dzus put it. She did believe that the operation should be carried out as soon as possible, however, despite the risks, because Tracy's condition was "too painful to do nothing."

It was clear that Tracy's life was deteriorating, and the prospects for improvement any time soon were non-existent. The hip operation would not relieve pain immediately, and in fact would temporarily increase it. Perhaps in a year this source of pain would be diminished, but by then what else would go wrong? If the other hip was gone by that time, there would be another operation on that one, and an increase in pain, perhaps for another year. And then what?

Along with the deterioration was the ongoing issue of inadequate pain medication. While most people going through an operation such as the one proposed for Tracy could have their pain eased with powerful drugs, the uncomprehending Tracy would, for the most part, just have to bear it. The anticonvulsant she took to control her seizures would likely interact with any strong pain medication, probably causing her to choke on her own secretions.

So Laura Latimer, on October 12, 1993, learned that her daughter's difficult, pain-filled life would get worse for at least a year, with prospects beyond that that were not at all hopeful, except that by then one hip might give her less pain. Laura went home to give her husband the bad news. He had been working in the fields all day and did not come in until dark. They had dinner, but the kids and a worker who had been helping Robert were around, so Laura had no real chance to talk to her husband about what she had learned from Dr. Dzus until they went to bed that night.

"He was horrified," Laura reported. "We held each other, and we cried. I said to him that really I thought it would be better for Tracy if she died, it would be the best thing for her. I told him I wished we could call Dr. Jack Kevorkian." Robert listened silently. When Laura was asked later if she and her husband had discussed Dr. Kevorkian any further, she said, "No."

CHAPTER 2
THE DECISION

No one disputed that both wife and husband had worked hard and conscientiously for twelve years to be good parents. Dr. Dzus described the manner in which the Latimers had taken care of Tracy throughout her life by saying: "I had no concerns about the way Tracy was being cared for. I think she came from a very caring, loving environment that looked out for Tracy." She acknowledged that the Latimers always had Tracy's best interests at heart.

And later, when the judicial system got involved in the Latimers' lives, two justices repeated much the same thing. Justice G. E. Noble wrote: "Not only [Latimer's] wife but his sisters described his love and devotion to this child. When asked about the standard of care the Latimers provided Tracy her doctor [Dr. Kemp] said 'excellent.' So the evidence does not suggest that Mr. Latimer did not do his share in caring for Tracy so far as his other responsibilities to his farm and family would allow him. He came across as a devoted family man with a loving and caring nature…" Justice E. D. Bayda, the Chief Justice of Saskatchewan, wrote: "[Latimer] was a nurturing, caring, giving, respectful, law-abiding responsible parent of the victim."

Finally, Robert himself said that cruelty to Tracy wasn't something he or Laura could ever tolerate. "The brutal description of cutting a large portion of Tracy's leg off was unthinkable to us…We spent years trying different drugs independently, in combinations, and in various dosages. We had to drive to Saskatoon very often, sometimes just for her blood to be tested to gauge the level of the drug in her system, and back the next day to see a doctor to adjust the dosage, or change to a different drug. We probably averaged two to four trips to the hospital in Saskatoon every month for the first three or four years of Tracy's life, mostly for seizure control."

Now, after twelve years of struggling to provide the very best care possible for Tracy, Laura and Robert were facing a terrible dilemma. The news from Dr. Dzus was agonizing. It meant more pain for Tracy, at least in the short run. And Tracy did not have much of a long run left. Dr. Dzus testified that a study at the Mayo Clinic looked at the survival rate of children with cerebral palsy with total body involvement like Tracy's, and only fifty per cent of them survived to their tenth birthday. Operations like the one proposed might make sense if the patient could be expected to live for some years, perhaps eventually deriving some benefit after a painful recuperation. But for Tracy these operations might well make her remaining time that much worse. And the Latimers were appalled by what they viewed as a proposal to mutilate their daughter. The idea of severing and removing leg bone, leaving a flail joint, was a violation of their sense of their daughter's human dignity. It seemed wrong to them. Could they refuse to accept expert medical advice? Could they be sure that the net impact of the operations would be worth it, for whatever "long run" Tracy had?

The Latimers both wondered about the wisdom of the medical efforts that had been made to keep Tracy alive. Alive for what? More pain? There were moments when Tracy seemed to smile and notice things, but even if these were signs of a low level of cognition, was it worth the pain she endured? Did the interventions, keeping her alive, simply amount to well-meaning but egregious torture?

Few people have ever been in a circumstance comparable to that of the Latimers. After that October 12 visit with Dr. Dzus, they were in despair. Their child's intense suffering could be relieved only by drastic surgery that they saw as mutilation, and even then her pain would not immediately abate. It would probably be even more intense for some time. And the same surgery would likely, eventually, be needed on the other leg. More than twelve years of struggling to keep Tracy alive and to give her the best possible life under the circumstances had come to this.

Latimer later told psychiatrist Dr. R. P. Menzies that after Laura made her comment about Dr. Kevorkian, he "said nothing, he pretended to fall asleep, but instead made his decision to put an end to Tracy's pain and suffering." Latimer went on to tell Menzies that over the next twelve days he agonized about the best way of ending her life, and "came up with carbon monoxide poisoning because it was the most painless."

Latimer knew what he had to do, but it was a daunting task. There was no law that could help; no euthanasia policy that would allow independent assessors to determine if Tracy's life was worth living. The deliberate taking of a life, whatever the circumstance, is considered homicide by the Criminal Code of Canada. There is no distinction made between taking a life with malice and taking one for reasons of mercy, although in the latter instance a case can be made (although it is a difficult one) for necessity. In general, two exactly opposite motivations for taking a life—hatred and love—are considered essentially equal under the law.

There were no friends or advisors to call upon for help in ending Tracy's suffering because anyone who did help might become implicated in the death themselves. So, as he considered what he felt he had to do, Latimer could not discuss his plan with anyone, including Laura. He did know, though, how she felt about the matter. She had told him that night after the visit to Dr. Dzus.

So Robert Latimer was completely alone when he set out on the mission of mercy that would have dire consequences for both himself and the rest of his family.

❧

October 24, 1993. It was an unseasonably warm Sunday morning in northern Saskatchewan, getting up to twelve degrees that afternoon. But winter was coming, and in a few days there would be a blizzard. Robert Latimer had been taking advantage of the good weather by working long days in the fields. But on this particular Sunday morning he stayed home with Tracy while Laura went to church with the other children.

There was nothing particularly unusual in his manner that morning. He was someone who rarely showed his feelings, although they must have been particularly intense that day. The idea that his life might change forever as the result of his actions must have at least crossed his mind. Yet he kept his thoughts to himself, and Laura apparently had no idea what he was planning. He knew he could take no one into his confidence because the legal consequences of being aware of his plans could be terrible. If Laura knew, she could be subsequently implicated. And anyone who knew— Laura or any other trusted confidante—might well try to stop him.

About eleven a.m., after getting Tracy up and giving her breakfast, Laura and the three other children left for church. After the others were gone, Latimer drove his blue GMC truck out to the old tin shed near the barn where he found a piece of hose, threw it in the back of the truck, and drove to his workshop. He hooked the hose up to some pipes and then put that assembly into the back of the truck, along with a hacksaw, and drove the truck into another shed, presumably to keep it out of sight.

Then he went back into the house and picked up Tracy, who had been sitting in her wheelchair, and carried her back to the truck. "I propped her up with rags…I covered her over, except for the face. I had to cut the hose with the hacksaw, hook it to the exhaust, put it in the back window…[and then] let it run."

He turned the motor on at about eleven-thirty. He climbed into the back of the truck and, sitting on a tractor tire that was in there, watched what was happening through the truck's back window. Tracy coughed a few times after about five minutes; then a few minutes later he thought she was dead. He left the motor running until about noon. Latimer checked her then, and she was limp. He drove back to the house and took Tracy's body back to her bed. Though she was gone, he put "pillows and things between her legs to place her hip." He may have done this in part to escape detection, leaving her as she would have been if still alive. But it may have been more than that: It may have been a grieving father carefully putting his daughter back in bed, one last time.

Some have called his action, in placing the body back in bed, insensitive and callous; but, like many hostile comments that have been made about him, that point of view itself might be considered insensitive and callous. For one thing, he probably wanted to ensure, as best he could, that Laura would never be implicated in the death; that it would come as a surprise to her. And he probably wanted Laura never to know how Tracy really died; that would probably be better for her. So he said nothing to Laura, and left Tracy where it would appear she had died naturally. From his actions, it appears that he hoped that he alone would bear the burden of knowing what had actually happened and that, if the police became involved, he alone would bear any legal sanctions for Tracy's death.

Laura found Tracy at about one forty-five, after returning from church. She yelled to her husband, asking him to call the hospital and the police. In describing what happened next, Laura said she "went to pick [Tracy] up, and her legs were relaxed, relaxed like they've never ever been in all her life, and it made me look at her again, and her face was an odd colour, and I knew, I knew she was gone, and I was so happy for her. I couldn't believe that it happened for her, I was so happy for her. I thought finally something has gone Tracy's way..." This was a mother who had for twelve years watched her daughter's agony; now, mercifully, it was over.

At about 2 p.m., soon after Laura found Tracy's body, Robert phoned the police—the Royal Canadian Mounted Police station in North Battleford—and told them that Tracy had died in her sleep. The police officer who responded to the call, Corporal Nick Hartle, notified the coroner, Dr. Kislen Bhairo, who agreed to meet him at the Latimer farm.

❧

Corporal Hartle had been with the RCMP for sixteen years. An unusually short man for a police officer, he lived in Wilkie with his young family. He happened to live next door to Bill and Mae Latimer. Hartle's children used to come over to get cookies from Mae. Hartle, in turn, had helped the senior Latimers on a number of occasions.

Hartle arrived first at the farm and found Robert sitting alone on his porch, smoking a cigarette. Hartle put his hand on Robert's shoulder and said, "I'm sorry for your loss."

"She was in lots of pain," Latimer answered.

Describing Latimer's physical and emotional state when he arrived, Hartle said Latimer was: "A little distant, a little distraught, very calm, he hadn't been crying, there were no tears, very matter of fact."

Hartle went to Tracy's room where Laura and the three surviving Latimer children were gathered. Laura was breastfeeding their newborn, Lee. Hartle offered his condolences and checked to see that Tracy was dead. He asked the family to come out to the kitchen, where Latimer was talking to the coroner. Hartle and Bhairo went back to Tracy's room, where Bhairo conducted an examination of Tracy's body. Hartle told Bhairo that he thought an autopsy would be appropriate and should be done. Seeing no obvious cause of death, Bhairo agreed. This crucial decision had enormous consequences for Latimer and his family. Without it, Tracy's death would have quickly faded into obscurity, and Latimer and his family would have got on with their lives.

Before he left, Hartle had separate talks with both parents, going over everything that had happened that day. During his conversation with Latimer, Hartle mentioned that they had decided to do an autopsy, the one word Latimer did not want to hear. He interjected that he wanted Tracy to be cremated, perhaps in his panic thinking cremation might somehow take precedence over an autopsy. Hartle said that was fine, but it would have to take place after the autopsy. Latimer had the good sense not to argue further, but he must have known, then, that the jig was up. There was nothing he could do about it.

Hartle's curiosity was piqued by Latimer's comment about cremation, coming as it did immediately after the mention of an autopsy. A child had died for no apparent reason while Latimer was alone with her. Hartle knew the Latimer family and the difficulties they had gone through with Tracy. All of this raised the possibility in Hartle's mind that this might have been, as he later put it, "a mercy type killing." Hartle might well have been sympathetic to Latimer, but that was irrelevant. He was a law enforcement officer, and he sensed that the law might have been broken. It was not his job to decide if what had happened was the right thing, as Latimer later described it, but whether or not something illegal had occurred.

Hartle questioned Laura after he talked to Latimer, and he asked her specifically about the idea of cremation. Laura was non-committal. They were talking in Tracy's room, and Hartle opened the door and called to Robert, who was in the hallway. He said, "Laura would like to talk to you about the cremation aspect."

At this point, the parents went down the hallway to the master bedroom, where they shut the door and talked for several minutes. Hartle said, "I could hear them talking but I couldn't make out what they were saying." Hartle went on to say that he walked by the door and back to the kitchen, and after several minutes they came out. Laura said, "Yes, we want her cremated." It should be pointed out here that Latimer has a different recollection of what happened at this point. He does not recall having a private meeting with Laura in their bedroom.

Hartle stayed on for while, as is RCMP policy; typically, they stay until some other support people arrive. He had helped contact some friends and relatives, who were on their way over. In the meantime, Latimer started to make coffee. As he was cleaning out the old coffee grounds, he suddenly became, as Hartle testified, "very nervous, very visibly shaken for a minute, and he dropped the coffee grounds all over—the old ones, all over the floor. Then he got down on his hands and knees, and began trying to scoop them up. He was having a difficult time with it, gave up on that, continued to make the coffee, and I turned the conversation over to just small talk on farming, and different things at that point."

This is a particularly heart-wrenching moment in the ordeal of Robert Latimer. Did he suddenly come to grips with what he had done to his family and to himself? It seems clear that Hartle was touched by the state Latimer was in and was apparently distressed by what he suspected was in store for him. In his application for a search warrant several days later, he stated that he believed that "Robert Latimer's motive was humanitarian in nature."

❧

The autopsy was carried out by Dr. Ranjit Waghray in Saskatoon on October 25. Hartle's suspicions continued to grow, and on October 27 he phoned Dr. Waghray. Dr. Waghray had some of his own concerns; he could find no obvious cause of death, although he could see some possible signs of carbon monoxide poisoning. Hartle asked Dr. Waghray to send a blood sample to the RCMP forensic lab in Regina and to earmark it for carbon monoxide content. As Latimer had feared, the blood sample led to the truth about what happened to Tracy. The blood was eighty per cent saturated with carbon monoxide; fifty per cent is life threatening. As soon as Corporal Hartle received this information on November 1, the RCMP launched a homicide investigation. Robert Latimer was the prime suspect.

Hartle spent the next few days preparing his case and getting a search warrant, and then on November 4 several police officers arrived at the Latimer farm. The weather had turned cold, and there was a lot of fresh snow. The first police officers to arrive that day were Sergeant Ken Lyons and Sergeant Robert Conlon of the RCMP's North Battleford general investigation section. They arrived at 8:28 a.m., in plain clothes, and rapped on the door. A somewhat disheveled Robert Latimer, wearing a bathrobe, opened it a few minutes later. Apparently he had been wakened by the police officers. The officers told him that they were assisting members of the Wilkie detachment in investigating the death of his daughter. He went back inside to get dressed and then came out and sat in the back seat of the police vehicle, with the two officers in front. Lyons, sitting in the driver's seat, with Robert directly behind him, turned to look at him. Lyons said that what he was about to say had very serious consequences and he should listen very closely. Latimer nodded.

"You are being detained for investigation into the death of your daughter, Tracy," Lyons said, and then went on, "You have the right to retain and instruct counsel without delay. You may call any lawyer you wish. Legal Aid duty counsel is available to provide legal advice to you, without any charge, and can explain the Legal Aid plan to you. Do you understand?"

"Yes," Latimer said.

"Do you wish to call a lawyer now?" Lyons asked.

"Not really. No," Latimer said.

"You need not say anything," Lyons added, reading from a card. "You have nothing to hope from any promise of favour, and nothing to fear from any threat, whether or not you say anything. Anything you do say may be used as evidence." Then Lyons asked again, "Do you understand?"

"Yes," Latimer said, apparently unafraid of proceeding on his own.

Laura, in the meantime, remained in the house with the children. She insists that at the time of her husband's arrest she was still unaware of what he had done. Latimer knew that he was in a lot of trouble, but he comforted himself by thinking that Tracy's pain was now gone. He later said that the investigation, the questioning by the police, was not the hard part. He told Dr. Menzies, the forensic psychiatrist at his trial four years later, that he had not a moment of regret. He said: "I can lie in a dirty old jail cell easier than Tracy can lie on the floor."

Sergeant Conlon said that they would like to take Latimer to North Battleford for questioning. Latimer wanted to change his boots first, which the officers allowed, though they insisted on accompanying him back to the house. They had to do that, they said, because technically he was now in custody. The time now was 8:38 a.m. The three of them went back to the porch area and Latimer went inside to change his boots. Laura was standing on the porch with her new baby, and when her husband came outside again she asked him where he was going. He said he was going to North Battleford with the police officers.

"Why are you going back there?" she asked.

"Ask them," he answered.

Conlon told Laura that the station was the correct place to conduct this interview. She asked if they would be coming back at some point, and Conlon answered that they might be coming back in the afternoon.

Soon afterwards, Lyons, Conlon, and Latimer were on their way to North Battleford. They had to drive slowly because of the recent snowfall and icy roads. There was no conversation at first, and then Conlon and Latimer engaged in some small talk about crops and weather. Latimer did not appear, then, to be particularly emotional.

Shortly after they left, Hartle, who had been observing from a distance, went to the house with two other officers and knocked on the door. Laura answered. He told her he had something important to discuss with her about the autopsy results. He sat down at the kitchen table with her and gave her a copy of the search warrant. Laura and the children and Robert's sister Pat, who was visiting, were all escorted out of the house while Hartle conducted a search. Laura claims that she still did not know exactly what was going on, but by now she must have had strong suspicions. Laura, Pat, and the children were all escorted to the North Battleford detachment.

Latimer, Lyons, and Conlon arrived at the detachment at 9:15 a.m., and went into a private office. Lyons, sitting directly opposite Robert, went over Latimer's rights again. After he had finished, Lyons asked: "Do you have any questions at all about that?"

"No," Latimer said.

"Do you want to call a lawyer?"

"No," Latimer said, shaking his head.

Lyons went on to explain that, while they empathized with Latimer, "we have no choice but to do the job we have to do." He said they would do everything they could to help him get through "this situation." He said they had spoken to several people and "everyone said the same thing, that you are a very caring person, a good person. At the same time we know this was not a natural death." He went on to speak of Tracy's pain, then said, "Bob, after considering all that is known, I have no doubt that you caused your daughter's death."

There was no response at first, but Lyons noted that Latimer's "eyes were heavy, glassy with tears." Lyons went on to say that he knew Latimer did not want to do what he did, and that he knew Latimer loved his daughter very much. Latimer nodded in agreement.

"This is something you felt you had to do for your daughter, isn't it, Bob?" Lyons said, but Latimer did not reply. Lyons said that he understood this was very difficult for Latimer, and that he, Lyons, felt bad about it. Lyons continued, noting that Robert had been a loving, caring father who had acted out of love. Still Latimer said nothing. Lyons repeated what he had just said and added, "Isn't that right, Bob?" Still no response, but by now Latimer was close to crying. Lyons said, "That's what happened, isn't it, Bob? Isn't that right?"

"My priority was to put her out of pain," Latimer said.

"That's what you thought was right, wasn't it?" Lyons asked.

Latimer nodded, with tears streaming down his face, although without sobbing. After a little more questioning from Lyons, he went on to describe exactly what he had done. Then Lyons asked, "Did Laura know?"

"We talked about it," Latimer said, presumably referring to Laura's Kevorkian comment from a few weeks before. At this point Latimer was probably just trying to say that he was not the only one who thought Tracy's life should end. But suddenly Conlon interrupted and asked Latimer if he would be willing to have the conversation taped. Latimer said he did not mind, but he balked at having it videotaped. But then they could not find a recorder, so Lyons took the statement in writing.

Latimer had composed himself by now, although he did break down in tears a few more times. Lyons completed taking Latimer's statement at 10:55 a.m. The recorded statement reflected what had been said earlier, with some additional information about Tracy's condition and why Latimer felt he had to do what he did. Early in this session Conlon interjected again, still concerned that Latimer had no lawyer present.

"Bob, I want to be fully sure of this before going further, you could be charged for murder. Do you understand that?"

"Yes," Latimer replied.

Latimer went on to give a full statement about what he had done, how he had done it, and why he had done it. When asked how he felt now that Tracy was dead, he said: "It's better. Soon as Laura saw her she was happy for her. She was loose. She was always stiff and in pain, she was always awake and in pain." He was questioned again about Laura and answered "[Her feelings] were no different from mine, she just said she wished she could call a Jack Kevorkian. She never participated in any planning, just thoughts in general."

Lyons read the statement back to Latimer, and then Latimer signed it. In doing so he signed away several avenues of defence. Although Lyons and Conlon were scrupulous in telling Latimer about his legal rights, one wonders if that is enough. There is so much at stake in a murder case that perhaps not having a lawyer should not be an option. Suspects with any sort of legal sophistication would never have done what Latimer did in this situation.

Latimer was not legally sophisticated. Sometimes he went so far as to evince a disdain for lawyers, an attitude that did not help him at this point or in the future. Perhaps it was not exactly a disdain, but the attitude of a self-sufficient and somewhat unworldly and stubborn man, who felt he had done nothing wrong and could take care of himself. Criminals need lawyers, and he felt very strongly that he had committed no crime.

After signing the statement, Latimer was taken to a prison cell in North Battleford, which he entered at 11:10 a.m. In those few hours since Lyons and Conlon arrived at the Latimer residence, Latimer's life had changed dramatically.

Later that day, Latimer agreed to accompany Lyons and Conlon in a walk-through of what had happened back at his farm. They arrived at 2:15 p.m. Conlon told Latimer he did not have to do this, and if he did it would be used as evidence against him. But Latimer had no objections. When they got to the farm, Conlon went to brief other officers there. As he sat in the car with Latimer, Lyons said, "I appreciate how honest you've been with us. In all sincerity and fairness to you, I want to again impress upon you the seriousness of the investigation, and that you don't have to go through with any of this."

Latimer nodded and said, "I know."

"You know that any of this can be used as evidence?"

"Yes."

Lyons then told Robert he had the right to call a lawyer for advice at any time and asked him if he wanted to call one before the walk-through.

"No, I don't," Latimer said, shaking his head.

They then proceeded with the videotaped walk-through, where Latimer revealed in detail everything he had done in ending Tracy's life. At 2:56 p.m., Lyons, Conlon, and Latimer set out to return to North Battleford; Lyons and Conlon to their homes, Latimer to his jail cell.

On the way back, Lyons asked Latimer again about getting a lawyer, saying it was up to him, but that it might be in his best interests to have someone speak on his behalf. Latimer seemed to be completely unaware of how legal proceedings worked, but at last did seem to hear the message that Lyons and Conlon had so desperately been trying to give him—although still in a rather unworldly way. He mentioned a local lawyer he had worked with on some land deals and said he would give it more thought.

When they arrived in North Battleford, Lyons tried one more time.

"Do you want to call a counsel now?" Lyons asked.

"You mean a lawyer?" Latimer asked.

"Yes," Lyons said.

Latimer said he would do it after speaking to his wife, but it was Lyons who, later that afternoon, ended up calling the lawyer Latimer had mentioned—Murray Greenwood. Greenwood was not in his office, but Lyons left a message for him. Later in the afternoon, Lyons and Conlon again took Latimer from his cell and went over some details about how Latimer had attached the hose to the car. During this meeting Greenwood returned Lyons's call. Latimer spoke to him in private for five minutes and then returned to his cell. No doubt Greenwood had told Latimer that he would not be the right person to defend him; that he would need a criminal lawyer.

The day Robert Latimer was arrested for murder, November 4, 1993, was the same day that Tracy had been scheduled to have her hip operation.

While Robert was taking Lyons and Conlon on a walk-through of events at the farm, Laura, the children, and Robert's sister were waiting at the police station. They were not going to be allowed to return home until Hartle had finished his work, which would be about four-forty-five p.m. Laura had a brief meeting with her husband about three-thirty, during which, Sergeant Conlon testified, he believes Latimer told his wife what had happened. Laura, however, says that someone else told her later that afternoon; at some point in the late afternoon, Laura said, someone told her that her husband had confessed to killing Tracy. She says she was shocked, although it is hard to imagine what else she thought all the activity was about. She also said she was angry with Robert for a few days, but became reconciled to the situation by realizing that it was the best thing for Tracy.

Latimer has been criticized for not coming forward immediately after his daughter's death. Today, when he is asked if he would have done so, had the autopsy not been carried out and the reason for the death not discovered, he simply says, "I don't know." He had a young family to be concerned about. He is a private man, and the idea of this story being picked up by the press and the life of his family being put on display was of great concern to him, as it is today. He felt he did what he needed to do and afterwards simply wanted to get on with his life—to be a husband, a father, and a farmer. Was this wish an avoidance of responsibility? Many individuals will assert that a person who commits an act of civil disobedience should submit himself to the appropriate punishment immediately afterwards. But how many of us would actually do so in a circumstance like Latimer's? It is easy to say, but difficult to do.

And this was not an act of civil disobedience. Latimer was not and still is not on a crusade to legalize euthanasia or to defend the idea of civil disobedience. In his view, nothing is wrong with the law on euthanasia as it stands, just with how it was administered in his case. Latimer is not a particularly reflective man; he simply did what he felt he had to do. At the time of this writing, he remains fully convinced that he did the right thing and is guilty of no crime. "The legal system can punish me if it wants to," he has said on many occasions, stating he would do the same thing again if the circumstances were the same. He acted regardless of the consequences, because it had to be done "for Tracy," but he is not someone who would have jeopardized his future or that of his family to stand on an abstract principle, even if that principle had meaning or significance for him. He is a practical man, not a philosopher or a crusader. His practical nature undoubtedly helped him take action, but it was not very helpful to him in responding to the complexities of the subsequent legal proceedings, even on so basic a point as getting legal help.

The Latimers' story quickly became a sensational one and, to his great distress, drew extensive media attention. He particularly dislikes having his family subjected to public attention. But the media coverage was relentless, and Tracy's death quickly became Canada's best known and most controversial case of "mercy killing."

Every major newspaper in the country carried the story and continued to cover it through all the trials and appeals, and then through Latimer's subsequent interactions with the National Parole Board. His story has been followed closely by magazines, including *Maclean's*, and by television news organizations. Countless letters to the editor have been published about him, as have many op-ed pieces and articles of various sorts. Even at the time of this writing, seventeen years after Tracy died, news about Latimer is published across the country at every possible opportunity. And he does not like it any more now than he did at the beginning.

Despite widespread public sympathy, there was also very loud condemnation, largely from certain religious communities and from advocacy groups for the disabled. Though polls have consistently shown that the critics are expressing a minority opinion, they make up for their low numbers with loud determination. Their opinion is that Latimer is simply a murderer who took the life of a defenceless child, and that if he is not punished severely it will become "open season on the disabled." Latimer's supporters, on the other hand, see what he did as a selfless act of heroism, risking his own future so that his daughter would no longer undergo pointless suffering.

CHAPTER 3
THE TRIALS

After his arrest, Robert Latimer spent eight days in the North Battleford jail before being released on three conditions: that he not leave the province without permission, that he report to the Wilkie RCMP every Friday, and that he refrain from drinking alcohol. He remained out of prison until his trial in November 1994.

Latimer hired Saskatoon-based criminal defence lawyer Mark Brayford to represent him. Brayford, admitted to the Saskatoon bar in 1979, appointed Queen's Counsel in 1995, has become nationally recognized for his legal work, for his writing, and through his speaking engagements. Latimer had a lot of advice on whom to select to represent him, and many lawyers would have loved to take the case, but he selected the relatively young, charismatic Brayford.

Brayford started right in by questioning the admissibility of evidence from Latimer's unwise talks to the police before his arrest. By the time Brayford got to him, Latimer had already revealed, on videotape and in recorded sessions with police officers, every detail of his actions on October 24. This was going to be a serious impediment to the defence, so Brayford tried hard to block it.

Telling all had come naturally to Latimer. In one way, he was probably relieved when he was finally apprehended. The deception had likely been very uncomfortable for him, and if he had not needed to protect himself for the sake of his family he might well have been more forthcoming right from the beginning. The trouble is, prosecuting attorneys do not give those charged any credit for honesty. Honesty just makes their work easier, and they are ruthless in exploiting it. Unlike those who speak freely, the dishonest give nothing away. Brayford's options for mounting a case for the defence would be seriously limited if Latimer's naïve capitulation to police interrogation were allowed to stand.

Unfortunately for Latimer, his openness to the police did come back to hurt him. On September 27, 1994, Justice C. R. Wimmer, who would be handling the trial, ruled that the material would be admissible. He said Latimer had made an informed decision and that he had been well-briefed as to his right to counsel. The trial started on November 16, 1994.

Because the results of this trial were subsequently thrown out, I will not review it in detail here; but a few points are relevant to the next trial, the one that counted. Saskatchewan Crown Prosecutor Randy Kirkham chose to take the case himself and to charge Latimer with murder. The charge was technically correct. According to the Criminal Code of Canada, when one person kills another with intent, it is murder. Latimer did mean to cause Tracy's death; there is no dispute about that. Manslaughter is defined as death carried out in the "heat of passion caused by sudden provocation." Clearly, this was not what happened in the Latimer case. But Kirkham could still have charged Latimer with manslaughter, if he had chosen to; this is a device sometimes used by prosecutors when murder seems too harsh a charge or does not really describe the offence.

I asked Mark Brayford about why the charge had been murder rather than manslaughter. "In compassionate cases in other provinces," he said, "the Crown Prosecutor has often used a manslaughter charge to permit discretion as to what sentence might be imposed. Unfathomably to me, the prosecutor in Robert's case laid a murder charge, which then tied the Court's hands on sentencing to life imprisonment. The Court itself could not reduce the charge to manslaughter unless Robert were to have said that he was so upset that he did not know what he was doing. Robert is far too honest to lie in court about what he intended."

Kirkham, who had decided to take a hard line, was not about to reduce the charge to manslaughter. In fact, he seemed determined to demonize Latimer. During the trial he referred to Latimer as "foul, callous, cold, calculating and not motivated by anything other than making his own life easier." Later, the Saskatchewan Court of Appeal admonished him for such unsupported comments, comments that were contradicted by all those who knew Latimer.

In Kirkham's closing remarks to the jury, he said that murdering Tracy, "should be no different here in this case than it would be if he had murdered [their new] baby Lee, who was two to three months old at the time Tracy's life was taken. Why should it be any different? We would not tolerate this conduct or have, I suggest, a moment's hesitation were it baby Lee, Lindsay or Brian Latimer as the victim. Your decision in this case should be no different just because Tracy had cerebral palsy. It is not open season on the disabled."

Justice Wimmer told the jury that, if they found Latimer guilty, they could choose either first- or second-degree murder. He probably did this to mitigate, to an extent, the unreasonable harshness of a first-degree verdict. Thinking they had no choice but to find Latimer guilty, they chose the lesser verdict. It came as a shock to the Latimers, who could not quite believe that Robert would actually be sent to prison. In an interview with CBC reporter Amy Jo Ehman, some months before the first trial, Latimer had said, "I honestly don't believe there was ever any crime committed here." He never seemed to really understand the extent of the trouble he was in, because he was convinced that he had done nothing wrong. Although most observers had probably predicted the outcome, the verdict—the harsh reality of actually being found guilty—seemed to take the Latimers by surprise. Latimer had refused to consider a plea bargain, at any point in his trial, again, apparently, believing he had done nothing wrong and did not need to try to negotiate for his future. In retrospect, this looks unwise.

Latimer went back to prison for a few days, until he was released on bail on November 24, 1994, on a $10,000 bond posted by his neighbour Wilson Barker. This was the first of many instances where Latimer would go to prison, only to be released on bail pending appeal.

This time, the case went to the Saskatchewan Court of Appeal, where the Court was asked to rule on both the conviction and the sentence.

On February 23, 1995, the Court of Appeal, with Saskatchewan Chief Justice E. D. Bayda and Justices C. F. Tallis and N. W. Sherstobitoff presiding, heard the application to overturn Latimer's conviction or, failing that, to allow a "constitutional exemption" to mitigate the mandatory minimum sentence of ten years before full parole after a conviction for second-degree murder. Constitutional exemption is a mechanism for individual remedies in unjust circumstances that arise from applying the law. It applies when a person's rights and freedoms, as defined in the Canadian Charter of Rights and Freedoms, have been "infringed or denied." Brayford argued that the ten-year sentence was too harsh a penalty for Latimer's offence.

On July 18, 1995, the Saskatchewan Court of Appeal handed down its ruling, unanimously upholding the conviction and denying the appeal for a constitutional exemption by a vote of two to one.

Chief Justice Bayda supported his two judicial colleagues in upholding the guilty verdict, because there was no doubting the facts of the case. Where he differed was on the mandatory ten-year minimum sentence, favouring a constitutional exemption to reduce the time in prison.

Appeal was then made to the Supreme Court of Canada, which heard the case on November 26, 1996.

But on February 6, 1997, in an extraordinary turn of events, instead of delivering a judgment the Supreme Court ordered a retrial, because it had been discovered that potential jury members in the original trial had been screened by the police. This was found out only because Laura Latimer, during a casual conversation with a friend who lived in the area, had learned that Randy Kirkham, the Saskatchewan Crown Prosecutor, had ordered the police to canvass opinions about mercy killing among potential jurors, of whom there were 198 in the area. Thirty of them had been given a questionnaire asking their views on a number of related issues, such as what their religion was and whether they believed in mercy killing. Somehow, then, of the thirty people screened, five (according to Latimer) made it to the jury, leaving seven jurors from the remaining 168 who had not been screened. Such loading of a jury could dramatically affect the outcome, particularly in cases such as Latimer's, where a jury might be tempted to find him not guilty even though he might have been technically guilty. Even one person with a pre-established ideological or religious objection to Latimer's action could skew the jury's deliberations. Five such people would be even more problematic.

During one of my interviews with Latimer, much later, I asked him about this odd event.

"I wanted to ask you about the jury-tampering in the first trial," I said. "I understand that the police and the prosecutor screened thirty potential jurors and that five of those screened turned up on the jury. How did you find out about this?"

"It happened after the trial and while our appeal of the verdict to the Saskatchewan Court of Appeal was taking place. Laura had taken the kids to swimming lessons and was talking to a woman from the area who was on the list of potential jurors. She happened to mention that it was odd that the police called and asked her questions about her religion. She couldn't recall immediately all of the questions and later phoned Laura and said that they had also asked her views on mercy killing. We told my lawyer, Mark Brayford, who agreed that it was odd. A few weeks later, when the appeal was denied, Mark hired an investigator to look into the matter. The investigator interviewed three or four people and found that there was a clear pattern in the questions. It turned out there was a questionnaire being used, sometimes by phone, sometimes in person. We obtained a copy of the questionnaire and it was given to the Supreme Court of Canada, with our appeal to them. They then ordered a new trial."

Charges of obstruction of justice were laid against Kirkham in 1996, but in June 1998 he was found not guilty. No charges were placed against the RCMP members who were involved. Kirkham subsequently left his position as Crown Prosecutor.

Latimer is understandably embittered by Kirkham's behaviour and became embittered by Hartle's as well, particularly after Hartle's testimony about the discussion between Robert and Laura regarding Tracy's cremation, a discussion Robert claims never took place. Hartle, who had been a friend of the Latimer family, further annoyed Latimer and his supporters when he became very friendly, as some supporters of Latimer saw it, with prosecutor Kirkham. One supporter said that Hartle followed Kirkham around during the first trial, carrying his briefcase and going to lunch with him. It is difficult to know if this perception is fair, but it created a permanent rift between Hartle and Latimer and Latimer's friends and relatives.

From the comments Latimer made to me in response to my questions about jury-tampering and from comments he made to me at other times, it is clear that he knew an unbiased jury would treat him sympathetically. Yet he was less insightful about those in authority who were sympathetic to him. For example, when I asked him about how he felt about Justice Bayda, his response was cool. He was inclined not to like Bayda because Bayda had, in the appeal, supported the conviction. But overturning the conviction would have been legally very difficult, if not impossible. Latimer had ended Tracy's life and so, technically, he was guilty. Only the jury had had the right to deny the legalities, but they had not done so. What Bayda could do was signal his opinion that the severity of the conviction was unjust, and this he did with great eloquence, in his remarkable statement. That he would have taken the time to do this, even though his colleagues did not support him, was extraordinary.

Justice Bayda wrote:

The personal characteristics may be summarized as follows. The appellant [Latimer] is a typical, salt of the earth, 42 year-old prairie farmer, born and raised on a farm near Wilkie, Saskatchewan. In 1980 [1978] he married a British Columbia woman whose father was a banker also born and raised near Wilkie. After the marriage Mrs. Latimer joined the appellant in his farming operation and they lived their entire married lives on the farm. Four children were born to them: Tracy in 1980, a son in 1983, another daughter in 1985 and their youngest in 1993. The appellant is a devoted family man, devoted to his wife and his children. He is a loving, caring, nurturing person who actively participated in the daily care of the children and in particular the caring and nurturing of Tracy.

To better understand the appellant's nurturing characteristic, it should be viewed in the context of Tracy's physical and mental condition. She was totally unable to take care of herself. Her body was tragically disfigured and disabled by cerebral palsy. She was born "clinically dead" and needed to be resuscitated. She obviously suffered serious brain damage at birth due to lack of oxygen. Shortly after her birth she developed muscle spasms—seizures—and for a while had one every minute. Drug treatment reduced the frequency to a seizure every twenty minutes and later to five or six each day, every day of her life. Some seizures were light, others severe to the point where her whole body shook.

She had no use of her arms or legs and could never sit up on her own. She could sit up in a wheel chair. During the last five years of her life she could not roll over as a normal baby of two or three months old can. The muscles of her body simply could not be controlled by her brain. They tightened when they should not. As a result, her body became "twisted up". To relieve the tension of certain muscles and the pain the tension produced, Tracy underwent a number of serious operations to have muscles cut: the muscles at the top of her legs (so her hips would not dislocate), her toes, her heel cords, knee muscles and so on. During one surgery, stainless steel rods were put on either side of her spine to straighten her body sufficiently to relieve the cramping of her stomach and her lungs.

Tracy had great difficulty swallowing her food and in consequence it took a long time—and some skill—to feed her. Often she could not keep her food down and would vomit. The family kept a bucket for this purpose near her whenever they fed her.

It was necessary to keep Tracy in diapers at all times as she had no control over her excretory functions. She could not focus her eyes and was always cross-eyed.

Her mother assessed her physical development and her mental development as that of a two or three month old baby. [There were estimates varying from two to five months.] Although she recognized her mother and father and her siblings, Tracy could not understand her own name. She did not know the difference between yes and no. Her only forms of communication were laughing, smiling and crying.

The appellant often bathed Tracy, fed her, cleaned up her vomit, changed her wet and dirty diapers and generally helped care for Tracy.

Mrs. Latimer summed up the father-daughter relationship between the appellant and Tracy in this passage of her cross-examination:

Q. *. . . The—what kind of father was Bob to Tracy?*

A. *He was a—he was a wonderful, loving father for Tracy. He was always there for her. He loved her very, very much and Tracy loved him.*

Q. *Did you ever think that he had anything but the best interests at heart for Tracy—*

A. *Never.*

Q. *—throughout her lifetime?*

A. *Never. He always put Tracy first.*

The foregoing capsulizes the heart-wrenching condition in which Tracy found herself and the context in which the appellant's nurturing characteristic should be viewed and understood.

The appellant has no criminal record. He poses no risk to society and requires no rehabilitation. He enjoys a very healthy and wholesome reputation in the community...

The appellant did not commit an irrational, depraved, brutal, sordid killing having its genesis in and motivated by some base impulse or emotion such as hate, anger, greed, self-gratification, jealousy, selfishness or some combination of those vices, all of which are considered by people to be negative and destructive. On the contrary, the workings of the appellant's intellect and will reveal a mind conditioned day in and day out, week in and week out, month in and month out, year in and year out, for a period of 13 years by his disabled daughter's pain culminating in what appears to be at the very least a severe preoccupation or an obsession with that pain. This is evidenced by his first inculpatory words as he was questioned by Corporal Kenneth Lyons. The appellant broke down and blurted out what was likely uppermost in his mind. The words appear in the following excerpt from Corporal Lyons' testimony [not repeated here]...

And again when describing how she died he showed sensitivity and concern for her pain:

I asked: "She just went to sleep?"

He replied: "She jerked three or four times, she's had worse seizures. I thought if she cried I'd pull her out. She didn't."

I asked: "You didn't want to see her suffer?"

And he shook his head. I asked: "And what happened was exactly as you hoped it would?"

And he nodded: "Uh-huh."

At his trial after the jury came in with its verdict and he was asked by the judge if he had anything to say before the passing of sentence, the appellant responded:

THE COURT: Mr. Latimer, is there anything you want to say?

MR. LATIMER: I still feel I did what was right.

THE COURT: Yes, anything else?

MR. LATIMER: Well, my wife mentioned that it's not a crime to cut her leg off, not a crime to stick a feeding tube in her stomach, not a crime to let her lay there in pain for another 20 years. I don't think—I don't think you people are being human.

It is also noteworthy that the appellant resolved to kill Tracy on the day (12 October) he received word that Tracy would need yet another painful operation. On that very day the appellant received another important telephone call. The social worker who worked on Tracy's case offered, in effect, to place Tracy in a nursing home. The appellant obviously reasoned that while it may relieve him and the family from having to care for Tracy in the family home, the placement in the nursing home would not relieve her pain. The appellant therefore declined the offer of a placement.

Those circumstances are strong indicators that the appellant was obsessed with Tracy's pain. It is a fair inference and an important one to keep in mind that she was not put into her father's truck because she was disabled. She was put there because of her pain, something very different from her disability. She was put there because her father loved her too much to watch her suffer. While the killing was a purposeful one, it had its genesis in altruism and was motivated by love, mercy and compassion or a combination of those virtues, generally considered by people to be life-enhancing and affirmative.

As for the physical components of the act, they did not produce a violent, painful killing. The act showed no heinousness or abnormal or aberrant behaviour. Rather, the act was committed in a gentle, painless and compassionate way…The actor himself was not a murderous thug, devoid of conscience, whose life has been one of violence, greed, contempt for the law and total disrespect for human beings. On the contrary, the actor was a nurturing, caring, giving, respectful, law-abiding responsible parent of the victim.

Justice Bayda's informed and compassionate assessment, based upon detailed reading of the evidence about Latimer and his actions, stands in stark contrast to the ill-informed, highly judgmental, and seemingly vindictive views expressed by some of Latimer's critics.

❧

After the Supreme Court ordered a new trial in February 1997, eight months passed before Latimer found himself back in court once again.

This time, the official charge against him read:

> *October 27, 1997, in the Court of Queen's Bench for Saskatchewan, Judicial Centre of Battleford, Robert W. Latimer of Wilkie District, in the Province of Saskatchewan, stands charged:*

> *That he, the said Robert W. Latimer on or about the 24th day of October, 1993, at the Wilkie District, in the Province of Saskatchewan, did unlawfully cause the death of Tracy Lynn Latimer and did thereby commit the offence of second degree murder contrary to Section 235 (1) of the Criminal Code...*

The weather on October 27, 1997, once again was unseasonably warm, as it had been the day Tracy had died. Representatives of the media were there in force, as the decision of a mistrial had created even greater interest. Two of Latimer's sisters—Marj Mosienko and Dorothy Harder—had come to support him. Given the result of the first trial, they all must have been less confident this time, although they did know that, for this trial, at least the jury had not been preselected. They also knew that the initial Crown Prosecutor Randy Kirkham had left his duties while under investigation for obstruction of justice in the first trial. The new counsel for the Crown was E. J. Neufeld, who appeared to be more even-handed than his predecessor.

On the morning and early afternoon of October 27 the judge, Justice G. E. Noble, went through the jury selection process, eliminating a couple of potential jurors; one who was a reporter on the case, and another because he had a connection to Latimer. Then, without the jury present, the judge discussed the admissibility of evidence from the first trial—exhibits that had been accepted then. There was agreement on this.

Later in the afternoon the jury returned and Justice Noble made his charge to the jury, emphasizing that their responsibility as jurors was solely to be "triers of the facts," while he as judge was the "authority on the law." Justice Noble told them "you must take your law from me."

Prosecutor Neufeld then gave his opening statement, repeating Justice Noble's statement about their responsibility. "Just as you are the sole judges of the facts, he [Justice Noble] is the sole judge of the law, and you must take the law from him as he states it." Neufeld also went over the list of the seventeen witnesses he intended to call and summarized what he expected them to say.

It is perhaps helpful here to explain one of the key elements of Justice Noble's and Neufeld's comments—why they stressed that the judge was the only one who could say anything about the law. It is technically true, of course, that jurors cannot rewrite laws. But jurors do fully have the right to ignore the law if they feel it is unjust. Judges do not like this, and they often try to lead juries away from such a consideration. That is why Justice Noble cast the jurors' role as "triers of facts," while only he could say what the law was. Left unmentioned, and going unrecognized by most juries, was the possibility of their ignoring the law.

This was the only real chance of getting a verdict of not guilty. The jury would have to refuse to convict Latimer of murder, even though he was, according to existing law, clearly guilty. That is why Neufeld jumped in to re-emphasize Justice Noble's comments about this. Justice Noble's words were a reflection of judicial antipathy toward jury independence with respect to the law, but Neufeld's were to protect his strong case by warding off any inclination the jurors might have had to think that in spite of the law they should not convict this man, a train of thought that might lead them to render a verdict of not guilty.

Over the next several days Neufeld brought in his seventeen witnesses, all of whom testified as Neufeld had outlined in his opening comments, though in more detail. Police witnesses described what had happened from the time Latimer first called them to report Tracy's death. Coroner Bhairo, pathologist Waghray, and blood analyst Murray Malcolm all described their findings. Pipefitter Ken Jones testified that the carbon monoxide poisoning could not have come from leaks in the house. Family doctor Kemp and orthopaedic surgeon Dr. Dzus (in Dzus's case in written testimony from the first trial) reported extensively on Tracy's condition, testimony that might well have been seen as favourable to the defence. Representatives of the group home where Tracy stayed on occasion basically reported that Tracy did not seem in such bad condition, implying at least that there had been no need for her to die.

Mark Brayford was presented with a difficult case, indeed. He could not build a case casting doubt on the exact nature of the events because Latimer had already confessed to the police. And the witnesses for the prosecution confirmed all of it. What defence was left? Simply throwing Latimer on the mercy of the jury might well have been successful, because it is possible that a jury would not have convicted him of murder for what was arguably an act of love. This possible expression of the jury's right to refuse to convict was what both Justice Noble and Prosecutor Neufeld feared (for different reasons). But, as will be discussed extensively in Chapter 10, explicitly using this sort of defence had been prohibited by the Supreme Court. Juries can refuse to convict, even when the accused is technically guilty; but defence lawyers can't tell them about their right to do so.

There was really only one other possibility for the defence: pleading necessity. This is an accepted but very limited defence in common law. The rationale for it appeared in a Supreme Court decision in 1984 (*Perka v. The Queen*) written, ironically, as it later turned out, by Chief Justice Dickson: "A liberal and humane criminal law cannot hold people to the strict obedience of laws in emergency situations where normal human instincts, whether of self-preservation or of altruism, overwhelmingly impel disobedience."

That Court had gone on to say, however, that the defence of necessity must be "strictly controlled and scrupulously limited," and it must involve true "involuntariness." Three elements are required for a defence of necessity to be successful:

1. *The accused must be in imminent peril or danger.*
2. *The accused must have had no reasonable legal alternative to the course of action he or she undertook.*
3. *The harm inflicted by the accused must be proportional to the harm avoided by the accused.*

Dickson went on to write: "At a minimum the situation must be so emergent and the peril must be so pressing that normal human instincts cry out for action and make a counsel of patience unreasonable."

The Supreme Court and Chief Justice Dickson felt they had to allow for the possibility of not strictly obeying the law, but they clearly did not like the idea much and severely restricted the use of such a defence. It seems to allow someone to kill a person in self-defence, but not much else. It is rarely used successfully. This was a long shot, to be sure, but Brayford had little else to go on.

After all the witnesses had been heard, Brayford's first hurdle was convincing Justice Noble that he could even present a defence of necessity. Noble cited the decision by the Court of Appeal in the first trial that such a defence was not appropriate in this case, and of course he was supported in this contention by Neufeld. Brayford argued that a number of new witnesses had been brought forward at this trial, ones who had not been heard at the first but whose testimony supported the defence of necessity. Brayford argued not that the necessity defence would necessarily prevail, but that the jury ought to be able to hear it, and then they should decide. Brayford knew that he could not simply argue for jury sympathy and ask them to disregard the law, so he had to find a way to tap into jury sympathy without explicitly asking for it. The necessity defence, while not a good fit with the Latimer case, would give the jury a means of expressing their sympathy for Latimer. They could accept the argument of necessity as a means of finding him not guilty, when really they may have wanted to find Latimer not guilty because he was not a criminal and had acted not out of malice but out of love. Knowing that jury sympathy, not strict legal arguments, was Latimer's only hope, Brayford sought a way, a pretext, to allow that sympathy to find expression.

Justice Noble was uneasy with allowing the necessity defence and took a night to think about it. The next morning he told Brayford and Neufeld that he was going allow the defence, or at least hear what Brayford had to say about it in his presentation. Brayford was uncomfortable with this because it was not a definitive acceptance; Justice Noble could change his mind after hearing it. If he did, Brayford would have taken his best shot using a disallowed defence. That is actually what happened, and was one of the grounds for subsequent appeals.

Brayford was put in a very difficult position by Justice Noble's initial equivocation on the necessity defence. Brayford had in fact prepared two defence summations, one with necessity and one without. But without necessity, and without the disallowed simple plea for sympathy and mercy, one wonders what he could have argued. So he took a chance with necessity.

Brayford initially went as far as he could, in emphasizing that the jury had the power to decide guilt or innocence, without telling them they could disregard the law if they so wished. Given the restrictions in the Supreme Court edict mentioned above, he wanted to stress the jury's power to decide. Justice Noble would subsequently undercut this as much as he could, by insisting that the jury had to follow the law. (This, incidentally, is highly debatable, though similar claims are often made by the judiciary.)

It was a tightrope act for Brayford to get the jury to disregard the letter of the law, while not inviting them specifically to do so. He referred back to witnesses, including prosecution witnesses, who had spoken highly of Latimer's character, of his long-time devotion to caring for Tracy, and of his motivation for what he did: Tracy's desperate condition and hopeless prospects. He used Latimer's legal naïveté as indication of Latimer's sincerity and honesty. He quoted from a televised interview Latimer had given to the CBC before the trials started. Latimer said: "I don't necessarily agree with Mark Brayford's way of handling this, but in the end I do, because I am totally lost in these matters, and you have to go with the lawyer, basically, when you're in court."

Brayford argued that this "fish out of water" aspect also was apparent not only in the Latimers' dealings with the law but also in medical matters. He was painting a picture of Latimer as an innocent thrown into a situation he was not well equipped to handle, both in dealing with Tracy's condition and in the subsequent legal proceedings. This is not a criminal, Brayford was in effect telling the jury, but a good and honest man in a desperate situation, a man asked to make complex medical decisions when Tracy was alive, and then complex legal decisions afterwards.

Brayford reviewed Dr. Dzus's testimony, which highlighted Tracy's pain and the Latimers' limited options. The pain necessitated action, but the operation Dr. Dzus proposed would lead to more pain and constituted something the Latimers saw as a "mutilation" of their daughter. Brayford went on at some length about the gruesome nature of Tracy's condition and how poor her prospects were. It was up to them, the jurors, Brayford told them, to decide what was *necessary*. They could use this, he was trying to tell them, to refuse to convict. He couldn't tell them that they could just refuse to convict, but here was an argument for them to appear to do so within the law. It was *necessary*.

But all of this strategy depended on Justice Noble and his acceptance of the defence. In the end, he did not accept it. He told the jurors—after Brayford had made the case in his opening statement—that it was not a legitimate defence. And it was not, of course, a matter of necessity as defined in the Perka case. In taking the defence away, which was probably the right thing to do from a legal perspective, Justice Noble dashed Latimer's only real hope and destroyed Brayford's only real option. In my view, Justice Noble erred, not in barring the defence, but in doing it after the defence had been made.

The case was not quite lost, even then. In spite of the straightforward case presented by the prosecutor—that the accused had, according to the law, committed murder—the jury clearly had enormous sympathy for Latimer. Brayford tried to build on this by calling four witnesses: Laura Latimer; two of Robert's sisters, Marj Mosienko and Dorothy Harder; and Dr. Robin Menzies, a forensic psychiatrist who had spoken to Latimer at length. Brayford wisely left Latimer off the stand; he does not perform well in such circumstances.

While undoubtedly eliciting considerable jury support for Latimer, presenting defence witnesses also of course opens up the possibility of damaging cross-examination. Prosecutor Neufeld did not miss his chance to do this and made extensive and unkind use of Laura's "diary" during his cross-examination of her. His intention was to raise questions about the claim that Tracy's condition had deteriorated after her back operation in 1992, thereby causing doubt in the minds of the jurors about just how terrible her condition was. The diary was really a log. Whoever was caring for Tracy would write in it, keeping a record of her bodily functions and anything else that might be relevant to her care. Laura had a habit of writing in "happy girl," perhaps reflecting Tracy's propensity for smiling when she was comfortable. Neufeld had Laura read that phrase over and over again as he asked her to read selected passages. But a mother's attempt to maintain a positive attitude should not be mistaken for a diagnosis. The comments meant nothing as an assessment of Tracy's true condition, which we can much better determine from Dr. Dzus, who clearly saw it as desperate enough to schedule an operation as soon as possible and who described Tracy's condition and prospects in grim terms. This was confirmed by other medical opinions.

Laura said afterwards she felt trapped by Neufeld's use of the diary. Tracy had been in such a bad way in the year before she died that her mother had seized upon any slight positive sign and written about it. A passing smile would be a moment of happiness for Laura, and lead her to record, optimistically, that Tracy was "a happy girl." Laura was shocked that these things would be used against her husband and her own testimony in the trial. And, of course, they were later trotted out by the extremists among Latimer's critics, who purported to have proof of Laura's mendacity and that Tracy, in fact, had been perfectly fine.

Maybe prosecutors need to harden themselves against any inclinations they might have to be empathetic, but Neufeld seemed to go too far. Laura had lived through a traumatic twelve years caring for her tragically ill daughter, and was now suffering through the trial of her husband for murder, yet Neufeld persisted in his lengthy and—in my opinion—cruel and unfair cross-examination. He talked about Tracy's smiles and movements as though they were intentional, rather than the responses of what was essentially an uncomprehending infant. He talked about Tracy "going to school" as though she were a normal child, instead of one who had to be sent to places like schools only for the stimulation, however rudimentary, of seeing new people and new places, and for illustrating the problem of severe disabilities to other children.

This tactic, however, appeared to have limited impact on the jury. Before rendering a verdict, they asked the judge: "Is there any possible way we can have input into a recommendation for sentencing?" This question showed they were wrestling to find a way to ensure that following the letter of the law would still be tempered with mercy. In other words, although Latimer was technically guilty and they thought they were obliged to find a guilty verdict, they believed it would be wrong to punish him too heavily for what he did.

Justice Noble told the jury that they could express their views on sentencing, should they render a verdict of guilty. So the jury, sympathetic to Latimer, apparently thought it could ask for a very short or even suspended time in prison. Justice Noble had given them only two options: decide the accused was guilty of second-degree murder, or not guilty. After four hours of deliberation the jury returned and the foreman, a tall, dark-haired man, said just one word: "Guilty."

Laura jumped up from her seat immediately behind the prisoner's box, slammed a railing and screamed, "No! No, no, no!" Her husband turned and went to her, embracing her and saying, "It's okay, it's okay." He was clearly shaken by the verdict, and later as he left the courthouse he said, "I thought I'd get at least one vote. But I guess not."

When the courtroom returned to order, Justice Noble dropped the sentencing bombshell on the jurors. He told them that, yes, they could make a statement about sentencing, but there was a minimum of ten years before full parole could be granted on a life sentence for second-degree murder. It was not something that he had just forgotten to mention. Before Justice Noble had answered the question about sentencing and without the jury present, Brayford had pleaded with him to explain to the jurors that there was a ten-year minimum sentence. But Justice Noble had refused to do so. And, worse, he had misled them into thinking they would have a real voice in sentencing.

Some of the jurors were very upset by this. A number of them put their hands to their mouths in dismay, some gasped, a couple of them cried. It is entirely possible that, had they known about the ten-year minimum, they might have returned a verdict of not guilty. Latimer might have been spared the severe punishment that now was about to be administered.

The jurors, though, were not quite ready to give up. They asked Noble to impose just a one-year sentence, in spite of the ten-year minimum. And, at the sentencing hearing about a month later, Justice Noble decided to agree with the jury's recommendation, invoking the constitutional exemption that had been at issue in the first trial. Essentially, his case was that Latimer's human rights were being infringed upon by a punishment that did not fit the crime. It seems clear, in light of Justice Noble's decision to argue for a constitutional exemption, that, like the jury, he had much sympathy for Latimer. He made a powerful statement in support of Latimer, noting his devotion to his daughter and family. In arguing for a constitutional exemption he added, "It is clear from the ongoing history of this whole case that he is not a threat to society nor does he require any rehabilitation. In summary the evidence establishes he is a caring and responsible person and that his relationship with Tracy was that of a loving and protective parent. On the evidence it is difficult to believe that there is anything about Mr. Latimer that could be called sinister or malevolent or even unkind towards other people."

Some of Justice Noble's decisions during the course of the trial hurt Latimer, but these can mostly be justified on legal grounds; he was doing what he thought was legally correct. Even his refusal to tell the jury about the minimum sentence can be defended by the legal principle that juries are not supposed to let the possible sentences influence them in determining innocence or guilt. His misleading statement that they might be able to influence sentencing was probably just an instance of bad judgment, rather than anything designed to work against Latimer's interests.

Judge and jury in this trial, then, agreed that, in spite of the mandatory minimum ten-year sentence, Latimer should spend only one year in jail. The prosecutor, however, brought the sentencing decision to the Saskatchewan Court of Appeal, where it was unanimously overturned by three justices who had not attended the trial and had not listened in person to the testimony. They denied the claim of exceptional circumstance and imposed the ten-year minimum sentence. This meant that day parole *could* be granted after seven years, but full parole would be possible only after ten.

The case then went to the Supreme Court of Canada, which rejected appeals of both the conviction and the sentence. High-profile Canadian lawyer Edward Greenspan joined Mark Brayford in speaking on Latimer's behalf, but to no avail. In a very unusual move, though, the Supreme Court justices suggested that although their hands were tied legally, they had sympathy for Latimer and he would be a good candidate for clemency. Clemency, however, was not something they could grant.

In July 2009 I asked Mark Brayford what was the first thing that came to his mind when he thought about this second trial.

"I just could not believe how the best justice system in the world could end up with such a wrong result," he said. "Worst of all, the chance of such terrible unfairness repeating itself is increasing, rather than decreasing."

When I asked him about why unfairness is increasing in our courts, he talked about how the power of juries is being undermined. In his view, the courts are undermining the power of juries to refuse to convict if the law is unfair in a particular case. He believes this is what happened in the Latimer case: it was not only that the jury could not be told of its right to disregard the law; it was misled about this by the judge. He also said that the threshold for cruel and unusual punishment, which was the basis of the appeal on Latimer's ten-year minimum sentence, was set far too high.

Brayford went on to say: "Then, to aggravate this situation, Parliament keeps passing more and more minimum sentences, removing judges' ability to exercise discretion in order to be more fair or lenient. If we trust judges to decide cases, we should trust them to impose fair sentences without tying their hands with minimum sentences."

CHAPTER 4
PRISON

I first met Robert Latimer, in 2005, at the William Head Institution, a minimum security prison near Victoria, British Columbia, where he had been since 2003 and where he would stay until he was released on day parole in 2008. At the time I was the editor of *Humanist Perspectives* magazine and, becoming interested in his case, I visited him several times there to get to know the man and to offer him support.

I had just covered the trial of Evelyn Martens in Duncan, British Columbia, where I happened to live. Martens had been prosecuted on two counts of assisted suicide, and although I had not before been involved in the right-to-die movement, I knew that humanists were interested in the topic and thought that my readers would appreciate detailed coverage. After attending the entire trial, which I am happy to say led to a verdict of not guilty, I devoted a full issue of the magazine to the trial and related issues.

I was fascinated by the trial, the issues that arose there, and the selflessness of this woman who risked her freedom to help people in distress who could find help nowhere else. She reminded me in many ways of the fictional character Vera Drake, in the Mike Leigh movie of the same name. Vera Drake helped desperate pregnant women in Britain before abortion was legalized; Evelyn Martens helped people who desperately wanted to die, even though assisting suicide in Canada can lead to a fourteen-year prison sentence. I was struck by the inconsistency of a law that allows attempting suicide but punishes assisting suicide. I was puzzled by the vehemence and viciousness of Martens's critics. The newsletter of the Euthanasia Prevention Coalition proclaimed, "Death Zealot Kills Two."

After completing my work on the Martens case, I happened to read something about Robert Latimer, learned he was at William Head (about an hour and a half's drive from where I live), and decided to visit him there.

One has to fill out an application to get into the prison and then be checked by security each time on arrival. Sometimes the guards took me over to a machine and asked me to wipe the inside of one of my pockets, or the side of my glasses, with a filter paper, which they then submitted to a machine that would detect any traces of drugs. Visitors had to leave their wallets, cell phones, keys, and any other things they might be carrying, in a locker. I had to plead to be allowed to bring in a notebook with a pen, something they would not agree to at first but eventually did. They would allow purchased food to be brought in—pizza, doughnuts, or other fast food—so I brought some in on a number of occasions, since of course Latimer had no access to such things in prison. Fast food has a strange appeal to those who cannot get it. Homemade food was supposedly prohibited, but that seemed to be one of those rules that was only sporadically followed. The guards varied considerably in their security concerns, although their default position was to say no. I found that if I persisted they would usually relent. One time it was close to Christmas and when I got there they said there could be no visitors other than family; there was some sort of party going on. But I pleaded that I had driven for an hour and a half to get there and that I had a journalistic purpose. After considering it for a while they called Latimer down to a room near the entrance gate where I was waiting, and we were able to have a meeting.

Normally we met in a canteen that prisoners were free to visit. It was a large room with a small food service area and a beautiful view out over the water, looking south down the coast toward Victoria. The prison occupies a spectacular thirty-five-hectare peninsula of land about a forty-minute drive up the west coast of Vancouver Island from downtown Victoria. In earlier years the land was used as a quarantine station for Chinese immigrants. Then, some years ago, a medium-security prison was built there, which was changed to minimum security several years later. The surrounding "treacherous" waters had once been touted as being like the waters around Alcatraz, impossible to swim through, but apparently federal authorities thought otherwise when they eventually reclassified the prison. I must say that the possible escape route seemed very unlike the truly treacherous one around Alcatraz. It looked like you could wade around the fence at low tide. The imposing double razor-wire fence at the entrance, extending along the full width of the peninsula and a little way into the water, is a holdover from the days of supposedly higher security. When the security designation was lowered, the fence remained at the request of nearby residents.

Latimer was not at William Head for the entire time he was in prison. Coincidentally with the start of Latimer's prison sentence in January 2001, Canadian Solicitor General Lawrence MacAulay issued an edict that all persons convicted of first- or second-degree murder had to spend the first two years, at least, in a maximum-security prison. This order fizzled out after a few months, or was conveniently forgotten by the prison system, which has a detailed process for allocating prisoners to available facilities. It seemed ludicrous to send Latimer to a maximum-security prison; he was hardly a threat to anyone. MacAulay went on to work his magic in other areas, and in seven months Latimer was quietly moved. Because of the timing—MacAulay's announcement came the week before Latimer went to prison—many people suspected that this was a punitive action directed at him. I asked Robert if he thought that was so.

"It sure felt like it at the time. But I don't really know. There were other cases that could have affected the decision. It turned out that it was not an effective thing. It interfered with the process in the Correctional Services for assessing and placing prisoners. I only stayed in maximum for seven months. It was another example of governments' trying to give the impression that they are getting tough on crime."

Because of the MacAulay edict, Latimer started his prison sentence at the Saskatchewan Federal Penitentiary, just west of Prince Albert. After seven months there he was moved to the medium-security prison in Bowden, Alberta, a half hour south of Red Deer, before going to William Head in 2003.

William Head is quite a pleasant place for inmates, who live in houses scattered about the peninsula. They cook their own meals and lead a relatively normal life, with various courses and activities available. They have television but no Internet access. Phone use is limited. They used to have a drama society, which produced plays that were open to the public. There was a small golf course for a while, too, but that was closed after people started to refer to William Head as "Club Fed."

I asked Latimer about life in prison.

"It was worst at first," he said, "but then is better once you become more aware of your surroundings. It takes time to get your bearings."

Then I wondered how the maximum-security prison was. "Was that the worst?" I asked.

"Every situation has its advantages. One thing about maximum security is that you get more chance to rest—something you need when you first get slammed into prison."

I urged him to tell me more about prison life.

"The food varies. It is quite bad in some places. Sometimes it is quite edible. We cooked our own meals at William Head. We had $30 a week to buy food from a grocery store and after a while you learned how to make that work. From what I was told they used to have open aisles at the grocery store, but too many things disappeared from that, so then they just took orders and handed you the food. The other guys in the prison were interesting. One famous bank robber would just light up when he talked about some of his bank jobs."

He was talking about Stephen Reid, mastermind of the infamous Stopwatch Gang of the 1970s and eighties. Reid had earlier served fourteen years for armed robbery and then, in 1999, years after being released, he and an accomplice staged a bank robbery in downtown Victoria that featured a high-speed vehicle chase through the city with Reid hanging out of the passenger-side window firing shots at pursuing policemen.

Understandably, Reid had some difficulty getting parole; a problem he jokingly attributed to Latimer. If they aren't going to let you out, he would suggest to Latimer, how are they going to let me out? He had a good point.

"I have heard that conditions are tightening up in prisons in Canada. Did you notice that?" I asked Latimer.

"There seems to be a general shift toward getting tough on crime. This seems to be a political line claiming to make the country a safer place. You see this in many ways in the prisons. Just a year ago an approved visitor could just come by and be allowed to see a prisoner. Now you need to give three or four days' notice. There are fewer courses available to inmates now—university courses seem to have disappeared at William Head. The food seems to be getting worse. It is harder to get passes for work outside the prison. I hear that it is getting more difficult to get parole—I think there are more retired police officers on the Parole Board now."

"How does all of this affect the incidence of crime?" I asked.

"Well the prisoners know about it for sure. I heard a lot of talk about the four-year penalty for gun-related offences. One inmate talked about how he was very aware that using a gun would lead to a more severe penalty. But he used one anyway."

"I have always wondered about the wisdom of bad treatment of inmates," I said, thinking about the closing of the golf course. "I know a lot of people resent any sort of kindness shown toward prisoners, but I just think that in the first place these are human beings, and secondly they will be out on the streets one day. And thirdly, some like you are not even criminals. How can brutalizing these people be a good thing?"

"If you beat the crap out of a dog, you won't have a very nice dog. A lot of serious crimes are circumstantial in nature—people get caught in circumstances not really of their own making. The idea is that harsher laws will crack down on, say, gang violence, but it just makes it sound like something is being done."

※

While in prison Latimer became obsessed with trying to correct what he believed to be an error in the prosecution's case against him. The defence case of necessity was that Tracy's pain could not be mitigated by strong pain-reducing agents because they would conflict in a dangerous way with the anti-convulsants that she was taking and that she desperately needed to reduce the number of debilitating convulsions. The prosecution claimed that there were effective pain-reducers that could be safely introduced through a tube into her stomach. Latimer claims that this was false—that there is no such medication—and he has wanted the decision of guilty to be overturned by the Supreme Court because of the presentation of this false evidence.

Latimer has doggedly pursued this argument for years now, in spite of the obvious fact that it is a lost cause. He has focused on this pretty much from the time he went to prison and continues to do so today. One of the reasons he went to Ottawa in early 2008, after he was granted day parole, was that he thought he could pursue this matter more effectively there, and he thought he might find sympathetic politicians. When he was not successful with this, he moved back to a halfway house in Victoria in 2009, presumably to a more agreeable climate. But he has still not given up the quest.

Latimer wrote at least seventeen letters to the Supreme Court between 2001 and 2007 (while he was in prison). He also wrote at least twice to the Prime Minister of Canada, nine times to various justice ministers, and six times to other politicians. The letters were sometimes angry in tone, sometimes sarcastic, and very repetitive in demanding the identification of the "more effective pain medication" that might have allowed "better pain management." Latimer repeats both of these phrases, over and over again, in his insistence that there should be some sort of reconsideration of his sentence.

But his request for reconsideration was explicitly denied by the Supreme Court on May 14, 2002, following a detailed "Memorandum of Argument" from the Office of the Saskatchewan Attorney General on April 4, 2002, which addressed Latimer's concerns and recommended against going further with them. Though Latimer continues to claim that no one is willing to tell him what the more effective pain medication would be, the Saskatchewan Attorney General's analysis deals specifically with this matter, saying that it was not some unknown drug that was being alluded to in the Court's decision, but a more effective means of administering known pain killers, through a feeding tube inserted into Tracy's stomach. Moreover, the main strategy to control Tracy's pain was not medication but surgery. It was the Court's understanding that this would eventually alleviate at least some of Tracy's pain; and that, more than anything else, undercut the argument of necessity. Even if it were shown that the prosecution erred in presenting the case for "more effective pain management," the case for necessity still would not be there.

Latimer has nothing to gain from pursuing this defence; it is futile—a pipe dream. Einstein famously said that insanity is doing the same thing over and over again and expecting different results. Latimer is by no means insane; the forensic psychiatrist who evaluated him, Dr. Menzies, said that he "found no evidence of any degree of serious mental disorder," and he spoke highly of Latimer's honesty and character. "He struck me as being a candid individual, thought about things seriously before he acted, he wasn't impulsive, he wasn't prone to angry behaviour, [a] sort of salt of the earth type person." But he did add that "he's a fairly stubborn individual, I think he's single minded." And therein lies the problem—stubbornness, coupled with a lack of sophistication in legal matters. Latimer is certainly a solid person. Justice Bayda also used the expression "salt of the earth" in describing him in his laudatory analysis of his character. But he is a wounded man, and salt and wounds do not mix well.

It was not only his relentless pursuit of a lost cause that was questionable, but his tactics. There is no reason why he should be particularly skilled in legal matters, but one would hope he might have at least realized this and have hired someone competent to help him. But, because of his ingrained need to be self-sufficient, he tackled legal matters and decisions he did not well understand, proposed interventions (for example, by the Prime Minister) that were not legally possible, and ventured into many areas where he was out of his depth.

The tone of Latimer's appeals to politicians was particularly unfortunate. He used phrases such as "slander, trickery and deceit" which were phrases that prosecutors had used against him. Critics were "parasites" who "regurgitated" criticism of him. In one letter he accused the Supreme Court of "shirking its responsibility to understand the arguments before it."

It is not that a better approach would have helped him get anywhere with this cause—it was hopeless from the start—but a more elegant or sophisticated approach might have spared him and his family from further attacks of the kind that so distressed him. In the March 6, 2008, issue of *Maclean's*, writer Charlie Gillis slammed Latimer, who had just got out on day parole, for what he called "Robert Latimer's angry crusade." Gillis's fear seemed to be that Latimer had been transformed from a stoic farmer into a voluble crusader for euthanasia. Gillis saw it as very sinister that Latimer was about to go to Ottawa on day parole, fearing he intended a "renewed push to relax the laws surrounding so-called mercy killings."

But Latimer's sad and lonely quest is a very limited one, focused exclusively on what he honestly believes was an error of fact. Advocates for euthanasia would have loved to enlist him in their cause, but he was not, ever, the least bit interested in them. His is not an "angry crusade," but a clumsy and ill-advised attempt to correct what he sees as a factual error.

Latimer is not a man who easily absorbs and understands different points of view, nor does he easily take advice. He cannot be shaken off his determination to seek vindication through reconsideration by the Supreme Court, either by the Supreme Court justices coming to their senses, as he sees it, or by their being forced to do so by an attorney general or prime minister. He has some loyal supporters, one of whom has constructed an elaborate and detailed website on Latimer's behalf (RobertLatimer.net). But they do not contradict him. I was visiting him in prison one day when one such supporter was also there. This person made comment about how someone had said that something Latimer had written in one of his documents was a mistake. Though I rarely saw Latimer angry—he usually seemed very easygoing—he jumped on this remark, insisting that what he had done was right and necessary.

In reference to Latimer's action with Tracy, I once wrote about compassion as "the willingness to help others, especially the most helpless among us." In a very different way from Tracy, Latimer was helpless himself when he was thrust into a world he was ill equipped to deal with.

CHAPTER 5
THE PAROLE BOARD

After my early visits with Latimer I wrote one short piece about him for *Humanist Perspectives*. But I knew that his parole hearing would be coming up some time in 2007. Realizing our readers would be interested in the outcome, I began looking into the matter.

Parole hearings represent a key point in the administration of justice. In Canada we do not wish to keep people incarcerated for any longer than is necessary to provide some basic level of deterrence and to provide protection to the public by keeping dangerous people locked up. The determination of the appropriate time for release from prison is as complex and important—and as fraught with issues of fairness, justice, and protection of the public interest—as is the initial determination of guilt and assignment of sentence.

Yet parole hearings, in Canada at least, are conducted with shockingly less concern for fairness than are trials. Those making these very far-reaching decisions—determining whether or not a convicted person is to be returned to society—are political appointees who are not required to have any particular skills or background for the duties they perform. The essential question, a determination of the chance of re-offending, is one that cannot sensibly be made by unskilled people. A background in criminology with an extensive understanding of research in the field ought to be a basic requirement, as should legal training. While there is no such requirement for board members, most members of the Parole Board's Appeal Division are lawyers.

Moreover, in trials the participation of the accused in giving testimony is carefully controlled by defence counsel and normally only takes place if counsel thinks it will help the defence. In this way, certain sources of potential unfairness are avoided. For example, if the defendant's personal style would create an undue influence on the jury, then he or she is not allowed on the stand. At parole hearings, however, applicants are expected to speak for themselves, although they can have someone accompany them. Because of this, one would expect that Parole Board members would be skilled in assessing the relevance of personal style, or at least trained to understand that they are not competent to make assessments based on such factors. Unskilled people placed in a position of such heavy responsibility, who are unaware of their analytical limitations, are prone to making all sorts of unwarranted inferences: they may think they can tell when someone is or is not telling the truth, or they may think an apparent lack of remorse suggests irresponsibility or callousness, which they may use in turn to wrongly estimate the applicant's chances of re-offending.

In short, a position on a Parole Board is no job for a lay person. Some argue that, since lay people are chosen for juries, why not for parole hearings? But the circumstances are entirely different. The main reasons are that juries are under the watchful eyes of judges, and the accused is under the watchful eyes of defence counsel. Parole Boards and candidates for parole are essentially on their own.

But if Parole Board members were actually selected like jury members, it would be preferable to the situation we have now. As political appointees, parole board members are not only lay people but people who are indebted to the party in power. This is not an ideal way to seek disinterested justice, and one can only think that it has been allowed to persist because the convicted are essentially a forgotten segment of humanity; fairness for them is not a matter of much public concern. There have been attempts to reform the parole system, and to replace political appointees on Parole Boards with skilled professionals, but these lucrative appointments are prime patronage plums. Our politicians will not give them up easily. The result is an ongoing scandal and an abuse of political power. Change will occur only when we demand that our politicians act more responsibly.

❦

Robert Latimer's parole hearing was held on December 5, 2007, at William Head, where he had been imprisoned for the last four years of his sentence. He was eligible for day parole, if approved, after having been in prison for seven years. I attended the hearing, along with seventeen other members of the media and press and two observers from an advocacy group for the disabled.

During some of my visits to see Latimer at William Head in previous years, I had questioned him about his upcoming parole hearing. There was one point I was specifically concerned about, and that was remorse. One hears stories about Parole Boards wanting offenders to be sorry for what they have done. Folklore has it that remorse is the first step toward redemption. If this indeed was to be a factor in the hearing, I thought that Latimer would be in real trouble, because he was determinedly unrepentant. Would he now, at a parole hearing fourteen years after the event, be expected to say that what he viewed as an act of mercy, an act that had drastically affected the rest of his life, had been wrong?

In fact, the idea of remorse no longer has much credibility among experts in the field. Before the Latimer hearing, National Parole Board official Patrick Storey, in response to a question from reporters, said that the research shows that remorse is no indication of the future behaviour of a parolee. There are offenders, such as pedophiles, who are truly remorseful, who cannot help themselves and will re-offend. And there are psychopathic personalities who, without the impediment of conscience, can effectively play any role that will help them get what they want, including the delivering of a persuasive expression of guilt and remorse. I was encouraged by Storey's understanding of this, because it was clear that a requirement for remorse would be particularly unjust in Latimer's case. But Storey would not be making the decision. That would be left to the appointees on the board.

I also wondered about Latimer's ability to make a good impression with the Parole Board. I mean this as no personal criticism, because there is no reason why he should be an effective strategist and manipulator of people. These are not qualities that loomed large in the world in which he grew up, or ones which he values or admires. He says what he thinks and tries to avoid anything personal. But I had spent much of my life immersed in academic politics and, though not likely a better person for it, I do understand something of how to influence people and situations. I could see that Latimer did not. His reluctance to talk about personal matters, his failure to get legal advice or coaching for the hearing, his decision not to have (as is allowed) an assistant at his hearing, all seemed like factors that might hurt him. At least they might, if the board decided to make an issue of such things. It was really a matter of sophistication and judgment. Latimer was no better equipped to handle this hearing than he was to deal with the police when he was first arrested and declined to have a lawyer, to understand the hopelessness of the legal issue he pursued while in prison, or to react in a positive way to the Supreme Court recommendation regarding clemency.

And yet, none of this is an excuse for how he was treated by the Parole Board. If anything, his understated style and lack of political sophistication ought to have made the appointees more, not less, understanding of his plight.

Latimer's parole hearing was held in the same canteen where we used to meet. A table was set up in the hearing room with three Parole Board members on one side facing us as we came in. This is the usual number for these hearings, apparently selected at random from a dozen full-time and part-time Board members. Latimer and his parole officer sat with their backs to us, as is required. He was not allowed to interact with or even to look at the observers. I sat in the front row, directly behind Latimer about five feet away.

One board member, Kelly-Ann Speck, of Mission, BC, took the lead and made some preliminary statements about the process. She is regional vice-chair of the National Parole Board, and has held a variety of management posts in government. The other members, who said less throughout the process, were Bent Anderson, of Victoria, former Chief Constable of the Oak Bay Police Department, and Maryam Majedi, of Vancouver, a manager in the Office of the BC Attorney General.

This was obviously not a situation in which Latimer was likely to give a good account of himself. He did not look comfortable, nor when given a chance to speak did he do so with much confidence. He had been given no help in how to present himself to the board; in a trial situation, not only would he have had a lawyer to speak for him, he would have gotten careful advice from his lawyer on what to say if he did decide to testify. In fact, at his trial, Latimer's lawyer, wisely, had kept him off the stand and relied instead on testimony from the more forthcoming and personable Laura.

But here, at this crucial parole hearing, nothing. One could only hope that the board members would be sophisticated enough to realize this, and would not be unduly affected by his personal style. Whatever one feels about the Latimer case, I would hope that most people would agree that jail time should not depend upon one's ability to speak glibly and convincingly about one's own emotions.

The parole officer who had been working with Latimer spoke first, in a voice so soft it was difficult to hear anything she said. But it was clear enough that she was strongly recommending parole, because Latimer had received positive psychological evaluations, had behaved well in prison, had taken courses to improve his education, and was at little risk of re-offending. She was questioned on this by Speck, who referred to one psychological study that said that, faced with similar circumstances, Latimer could re-offend, presumably because he had continued to insist that he had done the right thing and in the same circumstance would presumably do the same thing again. The parole officer did not see this as a problem because she could see little chance that he would ever again be in a similar circumstance. It had taken twelve years of watching his daughter's progressive deterioration, twelve years of seeing her frail body wracked with convulsions and severe pain, twelve years of taking her for highly invasive operations, with another in the offing, for him to resolve on this desperate action.

Speck, though, was still concerned about the psychological report, and suggested that it raised questions about whether Latimer understood that he had committed a crime, accepted responsibility for what he had done, and showed due respect for the law. This line of thought became the main basis for Speck's evident discomfort with Latimer. To me, it just seemed like Speck was playing the remorse card, as I had feared. And Latimer's problem was that, as an honest man, he could not express regret for breaking the law, when he believed that "it was the right thing to do."

As the hearing progressed, it became apparent that a number of questionable things were happening. Speck's approach to the subject of remorse or, as she repeatedly put it, accepting responsibility for his actions, was problematic, and Latimer was not performing particularly well. But Speck is a person vested with and paid handsomely for playing a key role in our justice system, while Latimer is a man who is inexperienced in such matters, uncomfortable with personal questions, and unwilling to be pushed into saying something he does not believe.

The limitations of assessing a person's nature from an interview are well understood now. Studies have shown, for example, that most people have absolutely no ability to tell whether someone is lying or not. Yet Kelly-Ann Speck and her colleagues on the board seemed to be of the view that they could assess Latimer's character by the way he responded to their questions.

Speck began her detailed questioning of Latimer by asking him about prior difficulties he had had with the law, in particular the conviction for impaired driving in 1976. He mentioned that he did get into trouble a number of times in the seventies for alcohol and marijuana use. Then she asked him: "Was drug use and alcohol use a part of your life on a regular basis then?"

"A bit, yeah," Latimer answered.

"What happened after with your drug and alcohol use...?" she asked.

"I didn't get into too much trouble after that...I think," Latimer responded.

Speck went on at some length to grill Latimer about these and other early escapades in his life. Did she think that his behaviour as a young man in his early twenties, involving alcohol and marijuana, was somehow still relevant more than thirty years later? Latimer's muted responses did not serve him well in this or in later exchanges. In his first answer, he could, for example, have said that he was young and immature at the time, that his friends were all doing the same things, and that he was not proud of any of it, just as many of us are not proud of things we did in our youth. His remark that not much happened after that, "I think," was typical of his tendency to express himself in an understated manner that seemed to annoy board members throughout the session. A lawyer could have helped him with this, but of course he did not have one.

Speck then went on to ask about Tracy.

"So we have then the offence that put you in jail—the murder of your daughter...what role did you play in her care?...she was very vulnerable..."

Instead of simply saying that he and Laura shared the care of Tracy, Latimer was imprecise in his answer, saying things like, "I was her father." To Latimer that would have seemed like a sufficient answer to the question. He understood that a father's role is to take care of his child. But it did not satisfy Speck. I started to wonder what this had to do with the likelihood of Latimer re-offending, which is supposed to be the thrust of a parole hearing. The board seemed intent on retrying Latimer for taking the life of his daughter, but without the presentation of evidence and without defence counsel. Years of legal proceedings had already considered questions like these, with careful arguments presented on both sides, and now Speck was going to put Latimer on trial again, in a circumstance where he was uncomfortable, unprepared, and unrepresented.

"What was your attitude to the reality of having a disabled child?...I am trying to understand how...you and your family responded to her ever-growing needs...was it twelve years of misery?"

Latimer, in an increasingly strained voice, tried to respond to the many issues being raised.

"Yeah, I suppose you could say..." he started to answer at one point.

"I'm actually interested in your view—not my view—your view," Speck interjected sharply.

Latimer tried to respond with a description of Tracy's terrible difficulties, but Speck said that he was not answering her question and she wanted to know what his feelings were. Although Latimer is a man who obviously has difficulty talking about his emotions, she continued with this line of questioning, seeming to place enormous weight on his reticence, apparently believing that discomfort in talking about personal feelings was a reason for denying parole.

Speck proceeded to question Latimer on why he made the decision to end Tracy's life. She questioned the decision at the particular time it was made, saying the doctor's decision to have another operation seemed like only a "slight difference" in the kind of treatment Tracy would be receiving.

"You term it a slight difference?" Latimer said incredulously. "We didn't see it that way." He said that they saw the cutting of Tracy's femur as further "mutilation of a child who already suffered an incredible amount."

Speck, though, wanted to know more about how he felt at the time, and

74

why he made the decision when he did.

"Your wife went to the [doctor's] appointment...and so the next day was the day you killed your daughter..."

"No..." he answered, as he tried to remember exactly when the events happened.

"So how did you get from finding out from your wife...to the decision that you made?"

Latimer talked about the timing and his discussions with his wife: "She just said she'd like to call on Dr. Jack Kevorkian."

"So this was initially your wife's idea?"

"That was the comment she made."

"So how did you get from that expression of grief, on her part, of being overwhelmed, to your decision to plan to carry out the murder?"

"Oh, it took a few days...I can remember driving around in the fields..."

"So how did you decide on the means that you would use?"

Latimer responded to these questions at length, but he did not seem to be connecting with Speck. Then Speck went into a series of questions about his discomfort with needles, injections, and other medical procedures, apparently gleaned from the psychological reports.

"Do you think that this came into play at all in the way you came to view the medical treatment of your daughter?"

The implication seemed to be that Latimer might have killed Tracy because he did not enjoy the medical aspect of her care. Latimer said that he did not like these things, but a lot of people feel the same way. Speck went on to ask about the means Latimer had chosen, carbon monoxide, and then she pressed him on the events of that day.

"You didn't answer my question...how did it happen that day...walk me through the crime..."

Eventually we heard another voice from the panel, Maryam Majedi, who had been staring intently at Latimer during Speck's questioning. She said she particularly wanted to know why, after Robert and Laura had discussed the doctor's report, they hadn't talked to anyone else.

"My colleague asked you a question about why didn't you ask for any help for you and your family. You said no, you didn't ask for any help. When your wife came back and told you about her discussion with the doctor...and you came up with the idea to kill your daughter...at that time did you think about talking to somebody...getting some help...trying to find other ways than killing her?"

"No," Latimer said.

"Why not?" Majedi demanded.

The medical profession had spent almost thirteen years trying to find ways to help, Latimer replied, and her condition had continued to deteriorate. He described how her condition had worsened with each surgery. He described in some detail how she was in great pain from a dislocated hip.

"When confronted with the realities of the position she was in, we could see nothing else that could help...we could see no golden solutions to her problems."

But Majedi seemed unimpressed and continued to insist that he should have sought other options, other than, as she put it: "I am going to plan to kill her...and I will do it when nobody's around."

Latimer seemed unsure about what to say. "It was the best option for her...we could not ask her—she had no ability to talk...she certainly showed pain...we didn't have options..."

"But you don't know if she wanted to die or not; you never know," Majedi responded.

"I can expect that she didn't want any more pain."

"But you don't know."

"I can only go by what I would have wanted for myself."

Then the interview took a nastier turn. Speck returned again to her theme of what Latimer's feelings had been.

"You reached the decision...and found a way to do it...It struck me as a very cold way to do this, to take your daughter and place her in the car and hook it up and then wait for her to die...You waited, is that correct? What was going through your mind?"

His response did not please her. He said that what was on his mind was that a decision was made, and he had to act on it.

"So you were unemotional about the whole thing," Speck said.

"I wouldn't say that."

"What would you say, sir...You are here trying to explain your behaviour— you need to share with me what was going through your mind at this point."

"No one has really asked me too much about that..." Latimer answered.

In seven years of legal proceedings no one had considered such questions to be relevant, but now Speck did.

Latimer went on somewhat haltingly: "...it was a very personal thing...It wasn't like a big guilt trip. I still don't feel guilty. I still feel it was the best thing to do...What I was thinking was that this was the best thing for her. It wasn't, as you characterized it, cold."

Speck responded: "...it was...it was premeditated...you were not over-whelmed with grief at the moment...you made the plan in advance...it actually required planning...I'm unclear as to your state of mind..."

"Like was I emotional? Yes."

But this clearly was not the baring of soul that Speck was after. She wanted to know how long he stayed with Tracy afterwards, and then tackled him on putting Tracy back in her bed and leaving her there for her mother to discover.

"Your family is off in church at this point...you picked her up and took her back into the house...why did you let your wife discover her?...you had not told her you were doing this, and instead of saying she died in her sleep you let her go upstairs and discover it...what do you think about that? Was that the way to handle it?"

Struggling under the attack, Latimer said something about it being the easiest way to handle things. This response gave the panel members very little satisfaction. Although it was unlikely that they had ever been in any comparable situation (who has?), they all appeared to have very strong feelings about what exactly he ought to have done.

"You tried to cover it up," Speck continued. "The only reason the world knows about this was somebody did an autopsy and discovered she was poisoned. Until that moment there was a charade going on...there was no 'I am doing this for the greater good and I am taking a stand on the issue of assisted suicide,' or anything, right? There was somebody covering up responsibility for taking a life..."

"I understand your view..."

"If they hadn't done an autopsy would you have been sitting around on your farm all this time?"

"I have no idea."

"...it is important...all sorts of people do things like this...were you ever planning to take responsibility publicly, and say 'well now we've had the nice family funeral...and now I'm going to stand up and tell you actually I killed my daughter?'"

"I knew they were going to do an autopsy..."

Maryam Majedi, during this discussion, was apparently still concerned about the fact that Latimer had not told his wife that Tracy had died. I continued to wonder how this much-belaboured point had anything to do with Latimer's chances of re-offending, or why the panelists appeared to have no sense of how Latimer's actions in this regard would help ensure that Laura would never be implicated in the deed.

"My colleague asked you a question..." Majedi said. "I don't think I got your response...she asked why you didn't tell your wife your daughter died in bed...you didn't answer the question...you just put [Tracy] in bed...why didn't you tell [Laura] before she goes and discovers her daughter is dead... why didn't you tell your wife, 'Let me tell you she's dead, she died in bed'... what did you gain by not telling her ahead of time...?"

"It was just an emotional thing...I wasn't into talking about it. It was just a matter of getting through it all...there were other kids around...I understand how you can see it that way...it was just the easiest way for things to unravel."

Again Latimer was being chastised for not doing things in exactly the right way, with exactly the right emotions, by people who had never been in his situation.

"You don't feel you're guilty?" Majedi continued.

"It was the right thing to do," Latimer said, with a weary, frustrated tone of voice. "The law feels I need to be punished. We need laws and that. But if the laws allow mutilation of a child then someone needs to alter that thinking."

"Sir, I am not talking about the laws...what I am talking about is you and your wife—the mother of your child...This is the mother of the same child and you didn't tell her that you killed her, or if you did not want to say that, you did not want to get caught, that she died in bed...I just don't understand why you didn't talk to your wife about it..."

"I understand [what you are saying]...these are just very emotional things...I didn't have the ability to sit down and talk on a rational level...we had dealt with her [Tracy's] problems for many years...we both came to the conclusion that she had had enough...we were not going to allow them to do that [sever her femur]."

Finally we heard from the third panel member, former police officer Bent Anderson.

"The leg was not going to be amputated," he corrected.

"No, it would be a flail joint. A section of her femur would have been cut off."

Anderson then went back to the issue of what Latimer might have done if there had not been an autopsy. "How would you have responded?" he asked.

"I can't say," Latimer said.

Anderson asked why Tracy could not have been sent back to the group home she had stayed at for a while, suggesting that the problem for the Latimers had been the burden of care, rather than the suffering of Tracy.

"It would do nothing for her," Latimer responded, "she was only thirty-seven or thirty-eight pounds when she came back from the group home the previous time...she doesn't eat well for other people."

The interrogation from the three inquisitors continued with Speck once again taking the lead, with a series of extraordinary comments: "You said you would do it all over again...you have expressed some views of the law I find to be interesting...there are all sorts of people who hold moral views that say we'd all be better off if we could go and kill a lot of people...we don't see it that way...why are you different?"

"That I want to kill a lot of people?"

"Why do you have the moral authority to take someone else's life?"

"I can only go by what I'd want in my own circumstances...the laws become insignificant when there's something more important...the laws were less important than Tracy was."

"It is not about one person sitting around and saying what they've decided," Speck scolded.

And then, apparently not grasping the problem of avoiding a double prosecution, she made some disapproving comment about how Latimer should have planned things out with his wife.

"...she mentioned Kevorkian," he responded. "We talked about it...it wasn't in any way a snap decision. It wasn't as if we both didn't understand

[Tracy's] problem...I wish there was more understanding of her medical problem. Maybe you people have a pretty solid medical background...Are you doctors?"

"That's not actually relevant, sir."

"Yeah, but it's a big part of it...the medical aspects of it..."

"Do you have a medical degree as well?" Speck asked.

I was stunned by the sarcasm of this remark. Latimer's question about the board's medical qualifications was clearly an innocent one. I asked him afterward about his understanding of who board members were, and their qualifications. He assumed they were experts of some sort, maybe professional psychologists. Speck's retort, though, asking if Latimer had a medical degree, was made in full knowledge that he had nothing of the sort.

Latimer was somewhat flummoxed by this and went on to repeat himself about the laws not being as important as Tracy, adding: "This was not something like sitting down and killing this bunch [of people] as you described it."

"So there was an emotional component?" she asked.

"Yes, there was."

"...one of the things in the file...you have a great deal of difficulty expressing your emotions," Speck continued. "Is this an accurate portrayal?"

"Yeah, I feel it is a very private situation," he answered, mentioning how difficult this and all the public focus on his life were for him.

"You chose to make it public," Speck said.

"No, I didn't," Latimer answered.

"[You did it] by killing someone," Speck said. "When you took a life you [brought this on]."

"Well, okay..." he answered in a resigned tone of voice.

After some other comments, Speck returned to an earlier point: "The psychological assessments of you have said that you are not at general risk of violent behaviour...however they did feel if you were in a position where you had responsibility for someone disabled or not able to care for themselves the risk would escalate. When you saw that did you agree with that statement?"

"Well, we spent years with Tracy, from the time of her birth..."

"Are you suggesting that it would have to be going on for a long time for something like this to happen?" Speck asked.

"...it is something that endures for a long time...I wouldn't walk into a room and see someone in pain and decide they should be gone...[Tracy's] entire life was about what was best for her."

"So you don't think this would happen again...is there nothing to suggest that the broader society is at risk?"

"I understand your concerns...but any time there is a probability it is still there..."

Latimer's response here was awkward but honest. He was saying that if such a terrible situation occurred again, he would do the same thing, something he deeply believed to be right. But his honesty did not serve him well.

Maryam Majedi went back on the offensive: "Sir, to continue that same discussion, you told the psychologist that in the same circumstances, you would have done the same thing."

"It was the right thing to do."

"And if something like this happens you will do the same thing."

Latimer hesitated. "Well, I mean, something like this is extremely rare."

"And, sir, may I suggest to you that something happening like this is not quite rare. People get involved in horrible car accidents and they get crippled, people get cancer, they get a lot of pain, anything can happen to people around you that you love...you have somebody you love in pain...is that what you meant [by a similar circumstance]?"

After some interjections by Latimer, trying to explain the situation he had been in, Majedi went on: "I hope your wife lives a long time, very healthy, but she is someone very close to you. She can have some medical problems where she suffers pain. My concern is that you tell the psychologists that you would do the same thing—what are you going to do to your wife when she is right beside you in pain? Are you going to pull the plug because she is in pain and you think that it is the right thing to do?"

This reminded me of an infamous question that was posed to Latimer years earlier by a Canadian Broadcasting Corporation journalist. "Are your other children afraid you might do the same thing to them?"

Like that question, these ones seemed to blur any distinction between a man at his wit's end in dealing with twelve years of his daughter's escalating pain and someone who would casually pull the plug on a sick patient.

Latimer attempted to answer this last series of questions, but was not particularly effective in doing so. He mentioned that his mother was on morphine now. The point he was trying to make—inarticulately, to be sure—was that he wasn't about to end her life. But the panel took the comment in the opposite way; that here was a case in point.

"So in your mother's case, if the pain killers no longer worked," Bent Anderson asked, "and you and her are in the same room, is she put at risk?"

"I don't think so," Latimer answered, in the understated manner that had worked against him throughout the hearing.

"Why not?" Anderson asked.

Latimer tried to explain how Tracy's situation was different, but his words fell on deaf ears. The board members had come to the highly unlikely conclusion that Latimer was indeed a significant risk to the public.

Finally, Speck questioned Latimer on his plans for parole. She expressed concern that he wanted to go to a halfway house in Ottawa rather than in, say, Saskatoon, which would be closer to his home and family. He explained vaguely that he wanted to be in Ottawa so he could investigate the prosecutors' claims that there was a medical option for Tracy that would have allowed her effective pain relief. The board, though, misconstrued this:

"So you are going to pursue some sort of advocacy," Speck said.

"I want to pursue the Justice Minister…and some politicians…" Latimer said, a little unclearly.

"You still want to pursue advocacy [rather than being near your wife and home]?" Speck said, incredulously.

Speck went on to question this decision, making it sound as though Latimer was abandoning his family in some sort of crusade in support of euthanasia. If it was not their intention to characterize him in this way, it was what the two observers at the hearing, Rory Summers and Laney Bryenton, representing The British Columbia Association of Community Living, took away from this exchange. In their responses, during a media scrum after the verdict was released, they mentioned, disparagingly, how Latimer wanted to go to Ottawa to be an advocate.

But this was an erroneous perception. Latimer sought only what he perceived to be justice for himself and his family. He never had any interest in crusading, or even advocating, for assisted suicide or euthanasia; he wanted simply to correct what he felt was a crucial error the Court had made in his case. It was quixotic, to be sure, but it was what Latimer thought to be the right thing to do.

At some point during this exchange Speck said: "I'm trying to understand how you are going to manage family support…" and mentioned his family and children. She was painting a picture of a callous man who did not really care about his family. Why did he not go to a halfway house in Saskatoon, she wondered.

Latimer commented that Saskatoon was still too far away from home to visit on a daily basis. But then, haltingly, he revealed why he really wanted to remain at some distance from home. He wanted to keep his family out of the spotlight.

"It's better to be away from family…it takes a toll on family."

But these were subtleties of emotion that were wasted on the board. We were led from the hearing room and called back for the verdict, in about an hour. The decision was no surprise to those of us who had witnessed the hearing. A few days later, I received a copy of the board's report, selected sections of which are reprinted below.

At your hearing today you presented [yourself] in a manner which demonstrated that you have developed little insight into the factors which contributed to the decision to murder your daughter. You could not or would not describe the feelings or thoughts underlying your actions at the time of the offence nor would you discuss the circumstances or dynamics of your family life. You appear satisfied with the position that you and only you were able to determine her life or death, describing such actions as beyond the law, a private matter exploited by the legal system…

You struggled throughout the hearing to provide any coherent explanations of your thoughts, feelings or beliefs…

…some of your replies externalized responsibility. For example you stated you knew your wife wanted to end her [Tracy's] life…

[You] reluctantly acknowledge you did not seek nor easily accept help from others, nor seek other medical opinions about your daughter's care…

You denied any connection between your personal phobias for blood or infections and your difficulties coping with the medical care required by your daughter.

When asked why, if this was the right thing to do you did not accept responsibility initially...you gave an inadequate response...you deliberately tried to cover up the crime by returning her to her bed, allowed your wife to experience the shock of discovering the body, and only came forward...after the autopsy...

You stated that you would do it all over again and when pressed for how you would respond where [a] life and death decision arises with a family member you suggested there was low likelihood that this would occur...when pressed about the reality that such situations are a normal occurrence, not an unlikely event, you struggled to respond...

The Board...was very concerned about your overall presentation and lack of insight and understanding...your overall inability or unwillingness to answer questions, your repeated reference to legally required mutilation, your continuing belief that you do not need to follow the law and your preoccupation with legal issues raises questions about your willingness to comply with the expectations of parole supervision or respect for the law.

In the absence of responses to questions the Board was unable to conclude there has been any commitment or motivation for change.

It appears to the Board that you require further intervention [imprisonment] to assist you in developing a better understanding of your motivations for this crime to ensure you are prepared to manage your risk for future offending.

It is strongly recommended that psychological counseling or appropriate programs be considered by the Correctional Service of Canada to assist you in this regard...The Board, after considering your file information and the presentation today concludes that your risk is undue at this time and Day Parole is denied.

At the time the verdict was released, there was a real possibility that Robert Latimer would remain in prison for the rest of his life. His position—that taking Tracy's life had been the right thing to do—would not change, and his personal style was not likely to change much, either. If he was brought before future boards like the one he had faced on December 5, 2007, he would be expected to say that what he did was wrong and to express remorse for it. That would never happen. Moreover, appealing the board's decision appeared to be a long shot. Very few appeals are successful.

Some of those defending the decision have claimed that remorse was not the issue in refusing Latimer's parole. For example, a representative of the Down Syndrome Society, shortly after the board hearing and following public outcry over the decision, claimed that parole was turned down "because he could not say he would not kill others in the future."

But this clearly is a disingenuous claim. Anyone who had followed the case could see that Latimer was no threat to anyone. It was disingenuous when cited by the board in its written decision and disingenuous when it was implied during the hearing itself. The utter improbability of Latimer ever again being in the same situation he and Laura had been in with Tracy ought to have been clear to anyone. The idea that he might kill his mother or his wife if they were feeling poorly, as suggested by the board, was absurd. One can argue that what Latimer did was wrong and that one ought not to break the law in any circumstance, or that there are religious objections to any form of induced death. People holding such views certainly have a right to maintain such positions and to argue that ending Tracy's life was wrong, regardless of the pain she was in. But it is absurd to claim that Latimer is a threat to the lives of others.

Once, my wife and I were asked to testify as character references on behalf of our friends' son. The young man had committed some unsavoury offences, but we thought he had pulled himself together and would be all right. Then the lawyer asked us if we would be prepared to entrust our daughter to his care. Put in those stark terms, the question made us realize that we had to withdraw. We could not honestly say that we would do that. Had a similar question ever been asked us about Latimer, we would have had no concerns whatsoever. Of the many people I have met who know him, none has expressed any doubts that he is a good and trustworthy man.

CHAPTER 6
THE APPEAL

A few days after the hearing, I talked to Latimer. Although as a reporter I had been stunned by the unfairness that was evident in the hearing, he was surprisingly sanguine about it. I had thought he might at least exhibit some outrage.

"I didn't expect much," he said.

This was a man who had been battered by fifteen years of legal proceedings and was weary of the whole thing. He did not think anyone in the system was going to do him any favours. He went into the hearing with low expectations about the outcome, and he was not surprised.

Outrage at the Parole Board's treatment of Latimer was, however, widespread in editorials, letters, and columns throughout Canada. There were a smaller number of opinions supporting the parole decision.

I was concerned about the injustice that this parole hearing represented. Whether or not one supported Latimer and agreed that he had "done the right thing," it seemed to me that what happened at the hearing was not right. We have a lot of people in prison in Canada, though not as many proportionately as the United States. If people are not a risk for re-offending, we want to let them out. Of course the Parole Board members claimed that Latimer was a risk, but that really was an absurd proposition. The board's performance at the hearing seemed so egregiously wrong that I felt something ought to be done to challenge them, but Latimer's reluctance to take any action discouraged me. Still, I contacted John Dixon, a philosopher and long-time member of the British Columbia Civil Liberties Association (BCCLA), who has often tackled cases of social injustice. On hearing the details of the hearing, he approached the board of the BCCLA and persuaded them to take on an appeal of the Parole Board's decision, assuming all costs, if Latimer was in agreement.

I went back to the prison to talk to Latimer, strongly encouraging him to take up the offer and assuring him he could not find better people to be on his side. He was reluctant at first, but eventually he agreed to accept the offer of help. Lawyer Jason Gratl, then president of the BCCLA, took on the case.

Appeals of Parole Board decisions go to the Appeal Division of the board. It is quite unusual for an appeal to result in a new hearing being ordered; this had happened only 116 times in 2,556 appeals in the previous several years. Much more rarely, decisions are altered directly by the Appeal Division. That has happened only nine times in the same time period, and most of those were not outright reversals. So the odds for a new hearing did not look good. But the case did.

One further cause for hope was that, as mentioned earlier, members of the Appeal Division of the board differ from regular board members in that most of them have actual qualifications to assess the reasonableness of the decision being appealed. At the time of Latimer's appeal, three of the four members were lawyers and the fourth was a psychologist.

Gratl's brief, submitted on January 23, 2008, was so compelling that it was difficult to see how any rational person could disagree with it. Gratl's case was based on three errors he believed the Parole Board panel had made.

First, Gratl argued that the board had failed to take the reasons of the sentencing courts into consideration. Gratl reviewed the Parole Board's explicit responsibility to take into account the recommendations of the sentencing judges and other relevant information from the trials, and then pointed out that there was no indication that this panel had considered the stated reasons and recommendations of the Supreme Court of Canada, the Saskatchewan Court of Appeal, and the Saskatchewan Court of Queen's Bench, or the recommendations of Latimer's two juries.

In Latimer's final appeal in 2001, the Supreme Court of Canada had clearly ruled that in Latimer's case "the sentencing principles of rehabilitation, specific deterrence and protection are not triggered for consideration."

Gratl pointed out that this meant that Latimer was "not being sentenced in order to promote the rehabilitation of his character or deter him from committing offences in the future or to protect the public..."

The Supreme Court instead said that the sole sentencing principle used in this case was that of denunciation, the objective of which is to "communicate society's condemnation of that particular offender's conduct." This objective, Gratl argued, was served by the initial sentence. The Court specifically denied there was a need for rehabilitation or a need to protect the public, considerations which specifically *did* appear in the Parole Board's written reasons for denial of parole. Seven years after the Supreme Court appeal, and after that body's due consideration of all the evidence and its recognition that Latimer needed neither rehabilitation nor to be imprisoned to protect the public, a panel of the Parole Board of Canada had taken it upon itself to impose these same rejected sentencing principles on Latimer.

Then Gratl quoted comments made by the Saskatchewan Court of Appeal after Latimer's first trial in 1994, in their decision to grant Latimer bail pending the appeal:

> ...there is no suggestion that Mr. Latimer is now a danger to society or likely to commit acts of violence if released. He had no previous criminal record, and apart from this conviction he has led an exemplary life without violence or lawless behaviour.

Gratl also quoted Chief Justice Bayda's strong statement of support for Latimer (reported here in Chapter 3) and Justice Noble's remarks following the second trial (Chapters 2 and 3).

Gratl referred to the reaction of the juries from both of Latimer's trials. The first requested "minimum sentencing . . . with parole as early as possible" and the second "unanimously recommended that Robert Latimer be eligible for parole in one year."

Gratl argued that the Parole Board had not considered any of this.

Second, Gratl asserted there was virtually no risk of Latimer's re-offending while he was on day parole. The Parole Board had erred, Gratl wrote, in stating that Latimer was at risk to re-offend. Such a suggestion, he indicated, was "contrary to all evidence" and "patently unreasonable."

Gratl went on to explain that the board's decision was based upon its belief that Latimer's lack of understanding of what he had done revealed "a hidden propensity to commit further crimes which in turn demonstrates a risk of re-offending..." However, Gratl argued, none of the available evidence supported this contention. He said that Latimer's action in regard to Tracy was a situational offence and it was very unlikely that such a situation would arise again. Gratl then referred to a number of psychological assessments that also indicated a low risk of re-offending. He added that Latimer was not like criminals who are subject to ongoing temptation to commit new crimes, and for whom it might make sense to wish to see expressed regret and a desire to change. Latimer was a man who had been forced into an impossible dilemma, and, even if the law insisted upon punishment for what he did, it was still a human tragedy, not a criminal act. Nor was it "precipitous." Latimer had provided nearly thirteen years of loving care for his daughter.

"In the final analysis, there is no evidence to support the conclusion that Mr. Latimer would be likely to confront such a situation if released into day parole."

Third, Gratl argued that the board had failed to consider supervisory restrictions. If the board was concerned about certain circumstances which might arise similar to those involving Tracy, they had the option of putting restrictive conditions on Latimer's day parole, rather than denying such parole altogether. Even though the idea of Latimer's being at risk of re-offending was implausible, and even though such concerns were not shared by "any psychiatrist, psychologist, corrections official, prison supervisor, court or jury that dealt with Mr. Latimer," the board could have addressed any such concerns by imposing a supervisory condition on his day parole. Such a condition could be something like:

> *Mr. Latimer is not to be found in the company of any severely disabled or medically vulnerable person, except with the written permission of his parole officer and under the supervision of two qualified physicians.*

Citing extensive evidence to support his position, Gratl went on to point out that Latimer had shown himself to be "a compliant and well-behaved individual," who would readily abide by any supervisory conditions the board might have set. Latimer had "never committed or even been suspected of a single infraction or act of disobedience in the 15 years he has been under the management of the criminal justice system."

In concluding his brief, Gratl wrote that "Mr. Latimer respectfully requests his immediate release by the Appeal Division into Day Parole." He added that Latimer did not mind if any special conditions were imposed.

"Existing law, Board policy, and available information," Gratl wrote, "unequivocally support Mr. Latimer's release into Day Parole…A total of 15 years have passed since Mr. Latimer ended the life of his daughter, and although the public debate about the status of his offence continues, there is no fact, policy or law that would suggest that Mr. Latimer should be denied entry into day parole. On the contrary, the incremental step of releasing Mr. Latimer into day parole is a mandatory and desirable step towards Mr. Latimer's reintegration into society."

Even though only a tiny percentage of parole decisions are even questioned by the Appeal Division of the National Parole Board, and only about one in a thousand is reversed, Gratl's brief led to a complete reversal of the board's original decision. On February 27, 2008, one month after Gratl filed his appeal, Latimer was notified that he had been granted day parole. The rapidity of the response was as rare as the reversal itself.

Clearly, the credibility of the original parole panel was left in tatters. Probably as a sop to the erring board members who had made the initial decision, the Appeal Division added the stipulation that Latimer, during his time on day parole, was "not to have responsibility for, or make decisions for, any individuals who are severely disabled." This is similar to what Gratl had suggested they could do if they were really worried about his re-offending. Gratl had also made it clear that, although Latimer did not care if such a condition were imposed, it would be pretty silly to do so. And so it was. Nevertheless, the Appeal Board insisted that "this special condition is seen as reasonable and necessary…"

Many Latimer supporters, and many of those who had been simply following the case, had been shocked by the Parole Board's initial ruling. Now Latimer was finally going to be released from prison—but it was more than that. For fifteen years our justice system had failed to find a way to recognize that mercy is not murder, failed to find relief for a good but stubborn man who was unable to do much to help himself, and failed to prevent one travesty of justice after another. Finally, in this long, tragic story, something had gone right.

CHAPTER 7
LIFE AFTER PRISON

I remember getting the phone call from John Dixon one morning in the early spring of 2008, a few months after Latimer had been denied parole, and some weeks after Jason Gratl had submitted the appeal. John was the person who, on learning in detail about the case, had won the support of the BCCLA for submitting an appeal. We were not expecting the Appeal Board to act quickly, nor were we even expecting a positive answer, even though the case that Gratl had prepared was very strong. We knew that very few appeals led to new hearings.

"He's out," John said.

"Who's out?" I answered, dopily. It was fairly early in the morning.

"Latimer, he's out."

I could not believe it. I had tears in my eyes, as did many others when they heard. It was not just for Latimer, who certainly deserved a break, but also for the fact that justice had been served, if insufficiently and belatedly.

He was not actually out at the moment of the call, but the one-in-a-thousand event had occurred; the original Parole Board decision had been overturned. It took a week or so to get Latimer's placement set in Ottawa, and for travel arrangements to be made, and then he was gone. I talked to Latimer by telephone before he left, and he sounded the same as ever, low-key but friendly. As usual, he was not going to show his emotions, if he could help it.

I talked to him again a few times in Ottawa. His sister Marj lives there and, when I phoned her, she said she was thrilled to have him back. He bought a bike and would ride out to where Marj and her husband lived. He sounded happy.

For reasons that I was never able to determine, after several months in Ottawa he applied to return to Victoria and arrived there some time in the late summer or fall of 2008. He didn't call, but eventually I tracked him down. I visited him in his apartment in 2009, and we talked about how things were going for him.

"You've been on day parole for about a year now," I said to him, "and you still have two years to go before getting full parole, when you can return home to your farm and family in Saskatchewan. How is the day parole working out, and how restrictive is it?"

"At first I had to go back to the halfway house every night, but now I have an apartment a few miles away and I can go there during the day and overnight for two nights on weekends. On weekdays I have to go back to the house by midnight and stay for at least seven consecutive hours."

"I find it odd that the halfway house is in the Salvation Army building at the end of Johnson Street in Victoria," I said. "That's probably the centre of the drug trade in the city. Why would they want to put recently released people there?"

"It's not ideal. The people who have drug problems find it very difficult. I just find it unpleasant. But where are you going to put these places? The people in nice parts of town don't want them."

"Can you tell me more about how the day parole is going?" I asked.

"It's going pretty well. I have some part-time work now, working with a local electrician. I was able to complete the first part of electrical training in prison and now need some practical experience before going on to the next level, which I hope to do at Camosun College while I am still in Victoria. [He did do so in the fall of 2009.] I travel all around town with the electrician, and I'm enjoying the work. My parole officer, though, has decided that I need to contact her from every location where we stop, even at coffee shops. I don't have a cell phone and it can be quite difficult to find a pay phone in some places."

Latimer was referring to work a friend and I had helped him to find in the summer of 2009. He worked with Victoria electrician John Arnold, who described Latimer as "a great guy to work with," and "a nice guy with [a] good sense of humour." He said Latimer would often get recognized; in coffee shops people would whisper that they thought that was Robert Latimer. Many people might have enjoyed that recognition, especially when most reactions were positive. But Latimer never liked the spotlight; it made him uncomfortable.

"Everyone feels for him," Arnold said to me. "I certainly do. He's gone through hell. He's very reserved, but very honest—no bullshit. He is eager to learn. Salt of the earth describes him perfectly."

I asked Arnold about the Parole Board. He said he had seen Latimer reporting to them a few times. Once when they were at a job in the Highlands just outside Victoria, a parole officer came and "gave him shit" because he was slightly outside the designated perimeter of thirty-two kilometres from the halfway house.

"Why would she make you do that?" I asked Latimer, about the requirement to phone the parole officer from every work site.

"Well, these people like to supervise you. She just added this restriction after a year on day parole. I had nothing like this when I was working in Ottawa, even working on a delivery truck, going all over town, even over to the Quebec side, in the first six months of my release from prison. This sort of thing is why I didn't want day parole in Saskatoon."

"Some people have wondered about that. I assumed that it was because you wanted to keep the public attention away from your family."

"It was partly that, but partly it was the parole supervision. I didn't want them bothering my family, and whenever you go home a parole officer has to talk to your family. This is upsetting for them. Even now, when I do get to go home for a few days each month, a parole officer has to go and interview my family."

It was distressing to hear that the Parole Board was continuing to treat Latimer like a criminal, that such standard operating procedures for real criminals were being used with him. As Gratl had pointed out in his appeal, the Supreme Court in its ruling on appeal had supported his conviction on the grounds that what he did should be "denounced," but had said that there was no need to be concerned about rehabilitation, deterrence, or protection of society. Gratl had pointed this out to highlight the absurdity of the punitive actions taken by the board in its original decision. It was not necessary, the Supreme Court was saying, to treat Latimer like a dangerous criminal. But the board, through Latimer's parole officer, seemed still not to have grasped this point.

❧

At the time this is being written, the Parole Board continues with its petty harassment of Latimer. He does not complain much and is allowed trips back to his farm every two months or so. During the fall of 2009, when he attended electrical contracting classes at Camosun College, he told me he was managing all right, but not doing as well as he would like to do. He was tired and the routine of returning to the halfway house on weeknights was draining. It makes it hard for him to study in a sustained way, though he is at least passing his exams.

He asked the Parole Board if he could be allowed to stay in his apartment on weeknights and return to the halfway house on weekends; a small concession, but one that would have meant a lot to him. This was denied. He appealed, through a lawyer friend, unsuccessfully. He appealed again and was denied again.

Another time, while he was in Victoria in 2009, Latimer asked the board for permission to visit his nephew Don Danbrook, who lives in Vancouver. Permission was denied on the grounds that a condition of his parole was that he was "not to have responsibility for, or make decisions for, any individuals who are severely disabled." Danbrook happens to be a quadriplegic who gets around in a wheelchair operated by mouth. He has been one of Latimer's strongest supporters, getting about amazingly well despite his handicap, travelling to vigils on Latimer's behalf and going to see him in prison in Victoria. Apparently, though, the Parole Board thought that seeing Latimer would put Danbrook in mortal danger.

❧

Decisions from the Parole Board seem to come and go and fluctuate for no apparent reason. Even permission to stay at his apartment on weekends has been altered without notice and remains unclear at this time. When Latimer returned from an approved visit home to Saskatchewan on a Friday night in October of 2009, he returned to the halfway house, as required on weeknights, then stayed in his apartment on Saturday night as he had been doing and assumed, having heard nothing to the contrary, that he could continue to do. On the Sunday morning he was picked up by the police who said he had violated parole. They put him in a cell in the Victoria police station and mentioned that he would likely be sent to Victoria's Wilkinson Road jail. But then he was released at the station and made his way back to the half-way house, where he was apparently supposed to be. Why did this happen? Apparently it had been decided that staying in his apartment on weekends had been, temporarily and without notice, rescinded.

The Parole Board explains its actions by saying that when Latimer returned to his apartment after an extended leave, instead of to the halfway house, they issued a warrant and took him into custody, and that it was later cancelled when he explained that he had made a mistake. The board claims it is troubling that Latimer has not been more diligent in under-standing the terms of his leave, especially since he already gets privileges "well beyond the norm for other offenders."

Such actions by the board seem erratic and at times gratuitously punitive. The requirement to phone in from every location seemed to just drift away, with no explicit notification or reason.

In the end, one has to ask: Why is this man being treated in this way? What does the board think he might do? Latimer is simply trying to rebuild his life, for himself and his family. He has been dealt so many blows that he is inclined to accept them without much protest. For that reason, it is up to those of us who are appalled by the fifteen years of shabby treatment he has endured to protest on his behalf.

❧

Some months after Latimer had returned to Victoria to serve out his remaining time on day parole, in the spring of 2009, I met him for coffee to discuss a plan I had been thinking about. It was to build up a case for clemency based on many factors, including his argument about the faulty evidence that he feels was instrumental in upholding his conviction. Not that I thought that was a good point, but we could make it part of a larger case for clemency, based on it and all the other reasons we could assemble. We could make a formal application with the help of sympathetic lawyers, maybe even Jason Gratl, who had written the brief that resulted in the over-turning of the initial parole decision. And, I said, we could make a public appeal, drawing on the widespread support he has across Canada. It was an excellent plan and, I thought, palatable to him because it included further pursuit of the matter he was focused on—the "more effective medication" issue. Both a structured application and a wider public appeal might well influence the politicians. Without clemency, I pointed out, his life sentence would mean that he would be on parole for life (full parole after three years of day parole), which would mean reporting to parole officers for the rest of his life, being constantly subjected to the possibility of further incarceration, having serious travel restrictions, and having a criminal record as a murderer. I knew he hated the parole officer's presence at his farm, because of his family's being there, and if parole continued (as it would, without clemency), parole officers would continue to monitor him, and probably continue to visit the farm, for as long as he lived. He listened quietly while I talked.

"So," I finally said, "would you consider this idea?"

"No," he said.

"No? You won't?"

"No, I won't."

"Well, would you at least think about it?" I asked.

"No," he said.

I subsequently found out that others in Victoria had also talked to him about this. Lavinia Rohas has a child of her own with severe cerebral palsy, and has spent many years of her own in coping with a problem similar to that of the Latimers. Rohas has become an ardent supporter of euthanasia and assisted suicide and feels that Latimer's treatment has been most unfair. Sometime before I had my unsuccessful meeting on clemency with Latimer, she met him to urge something similar. That meeting had ended with Latimer giving her an angry response. He did not get angry with me, but he was very firm.

Latimer's attitude toward clemency is one of the oddest aspects of his behaviour through the period of his incarceration and then day parole release.

Three types of pardon are allowed under the Criminal Code of Canada: a full and complete pardon, recognizing that the conviction was in error; a conditional pardon, that sets aside a criminal conviction and removes the restrictions of that conviction; and one that involves remission of monetary penalties. Pardons can be granted by the Governor General or the federal cabinet, and are done on recommendation from the National Parole Board. The board uses the following in evaluating applications for a pardon:

1. *There must be clear and strong evidence of injustice or undue hardship (e.g. suffering of a mental, physical and/or financial nature that is out of proportion to the nature and the seriousness of the offence and more severe than for other individuals in similar situations).*
2. *Each application is strictly examined on its own merits. Consideration is not given to the hardship of anyone else, and it is not considered posthumously.*
3. *The applicant must have exhausted all other avenues available under the Criminal Code, or other pertinent legislation (i.e. appeals, termination of probation, miscarriage of justice).*
4. *The independence of the judiciary shall be respected in that there must be stronger and more specific grounds to recommend action that would interfere with a court's decision.*
5. *It is intended only for rare cases in which considerations of justice, humanity and compassion override the normal administration of justice*
6. *The decision should not, in any way, increase the penalty for the applicant.*

And Section 749 of the Criminal Code also says: *"Nothing in this Act in any manner limits or affects Her Majesty's royal prerogative of mercy."*

One would think that if there ever was a case that fit these criteria and cried out for some level of application of the "royal prerogative of mercy," Latimer's is it. In the absence of other legal remedies, then surely this is the way to go. Although there would be political opposition, polls have consistently shown that about three-quarters of Canadians are sympathetic to Latimer, and it is likely that there would be widespread support for a pardon. Even for a socially conservative government there might be a political advantage in it.

The case for clemency is so compelling that the Supreme Court, in its final denial of Latimer's appeal, had made the extraordinary suggestion that it be considered. The Court quoted an earlier case, *Sopinka J.R. vs Sarson* [1996] in support:

> *Where the courts are unable to provide an appropriate remedy in cases that the executive sees as unjust punishment, the executive is permitted to dispense "mercy", and order the release of the offender. The Royal Prerogative of Mercy is the only potential remedy for persons who have exhausted their rights of appeal . . .*

The Court indicated that the decision was not up to them, but went on to say:

> *...Mr. Latimer has undergone two trials and two appeals to the Court of Appeals in Saskatchewan and this Court, with attendant publicity and consequential agony for him and his family.*

This was a startling show of support for Latimer, for a Court that had just unanimously turned down Latimer's appeal of his conviction. They were clearly signalling that their hands were tied by the law—that on legal grounds they needed to uphold the conviction. But at the same time, they were saying, this man has suffered enough for what he did. They were throwing him a lifeline. The wise thing for Latimer would have been to seize it and pursue it with insight, dignity, and vigour. He did not, however, do that. He failed to grasp the lifeline.

Latimer did make one half-hearted response. In April of 2001, a few months after he went to prison, he sent a hand-written letter to Lawrence MacAulay, the Solicitor General of Canada, in which he asked about the possibility of clemency. He wrote:

> *I am writing to you to find out if there is any substance to a Royal Prerogative of Mercy, a judgment or option mentioned by the Supreme Court of Canada in their Jan18/2001 decision to have me spend a lot of time in prison. I have not read their decision but have been told by my lawyer Mark Brayford as well as media reports that the Court did mention this option.*

Because I have been told of this option or chance at freedom, I feel I must make certain it will or will not be available to me now. My reason for wanting to know now is because of the farm land I own. I have to make a decision as to how and who will be farming it this year. I don't want to rent the land out only to find in a day or two that this Royal Prerogative of Mercy is a real thing and I am free...

I am hoping for a realization of this Royal Prerogative of Mercy, and that it could be done in time for me to carry on farming this year.

I don't want to seem demanding, but I would appreciate an answer as to the availability of this Royal Prerogative of Mercy so that I can best manage my farm.

The letter was almost heart-breaking in its plain-spoken and honest naïveté. Was a decision likely to be expedited so Latimer could "best manage his farm?" This sounded like a man who was still in shock over his imprisonment, who was no longer getting much advice, who harboured resentment toward the Supreme Court for not setting him free, and who had no idea of what was entailed in getting a pardon. MacAulay answered the letter and directed Latimer to apply through his lawyer, indicating that "applications for clemency are rare" and that "the consideration of such requests can be a lengthy and complex process that requires some time to complete."

Apparently discouraged by this response, Latimer seems to have given up on the idea, although it was a real possibility for him, and turned his attention instead to challenging the Court's decision. The passages quoted above and most of the correspondence are all posted on Latimer's website, as well as being in a 235-page hard-copy dossier that he has compiled. His discussion of clemency in his letter to MacAulay, and the response, occupy pages two to five in the dossier.

A few months later, I was again interviewing Latimer for this book. We were at his apartment and he seemed quite relaxed, so I decided to ask him again about his opposition to clemency.

"While the Supreme Court of Canada turned down your appeal of both the conviction and the sentence," I said, "they did suggest that your case might be an appropriate one for what is called the Royal Prerogative of Mercy—a means by which the federal cabinet can give clemency. This showed that they recognized that something was wrong with what happened to you, but rather than remedy it themselves, they suggested this other route. You have mentioned that it is not something you wish to pursue, at least not now. Why not?"

Latimer gave me a lengthy answer.

"There are a few reasons. When I looked into it, I found that you have to apply through the Parole Board. It is hard to appeal to them when they are the people who did not even want to let me out on day parole. And it is difficult when people in positions of power are being lobbied by religious groups and representatives of the disabled. Why, for example, would the Ontario justice minister, from a province that had nothing to do with my case, send a representative to my Supreme Court hearing to speak against me? They, along with religious spokesmen and someone representing several disabled groups, were allowed to speak as 'interveners' at my hearing. If it had been a football game they would have called a piling-on penalty.

"Even by the authorities' own numbers, I spent much more time in prison than the average federal prisoner. When I was in Ottawa I went to a presentation on the prison system hosted by Supreme Court Justice Beverley McLachlin. There were three panel members: The Ottawa police chief, *Ottawa Citizen* columnist Dan Gardner (who had written some good things about my situation), and a guy named Rob Sampson, who was described by the Chief Justice as an independent businessman. He is the author of the 'Sampson Report,' a report that was done for his employer—the federal government. This Sampson fellow clearly said that the average inmate's stay in federal prison is sixteen months. With my seven years mandatory, and an additional four months taken by the bogus Parole Board decision, I spent over eighty-eight months in prison. That is over 5.5 times the average stay in a federal prison.

"But there is something else. I have always wanted an honest answer from the Courts as to exactly what drug they cited as being 'a more effective pain medication,' or what was the 'better pain management available' to treat Tracy with. These bogus claims are the most crucial element of the Supreme Court's decision to uphold the conviction and life sentence. I have been writing them since I read their very flawed decision in 2001. Canadians have paid for all of these sneaky things, none more than us. Most Canadians want situations such as ours dealt with honestly. This religiously righteous, dishonest way of ruling against us, and doing so much damage to us, could potentially be directed at other Canadians. The Courts are there to serve and protect themselves, the police, and the prosecutors, first; then ordinary Canadians get what is left over as justice.

"The authorities would want me to praise the rightness of what they did to me, for me to get any form of what they describe as clemency. I would not be able to say negative things about what happened, and I have nothing but negative things to say. Am I about to come full circle and praise all the dishonest things that were done to me? Could I say that the courts were right and we should have carried on with mutilating and torturing our daughter? That I was mistaken in my judgement about this? They would not even allow me this at the Parole Board hearing, where the concern is supposed to be about public safety. It came out that in order to get out of prison I should say I was wrong and that the courts were right and we should have carried on with the mutilation and torture. And that we should insert a feeding tube in her stomach and administer a more effective pain reliever, even though no one can say what such a pain reliever would be.

"I'd like it if the courts would be honest about the medical claims they use against me. I will continue to point out the error about the pain reliever that was allowed to influence the decisions about my case. I will not change my position on this, whatever they want to do to me."

Latimer's comments reveal a profound misunderstanding of the idea of clemency and an understandable if debilitating bitterness about what has happened to him. I had been aware of his view about what clemency would mean for some time; it first arose when I was writing my magazine articles about him years earlier. Then, when he first got day parole in early 2008 and went to Ottawa, I had a few telephone conversations with his sister, Marj Mosienko. At one point I asked her to explain his attitude toward clemency.

"I think he thinks it is an admission of guilt," she said. "And he believes he has nothing to feel guilty about; that he did the right thing."

"But it is no such thing; it is an exoneration," I said.

"You will have difficulty convincing him of that," she said.

She was right.

102

Robert and Laura Latimer leave the courthouse in Battleford on November 3, 1997.

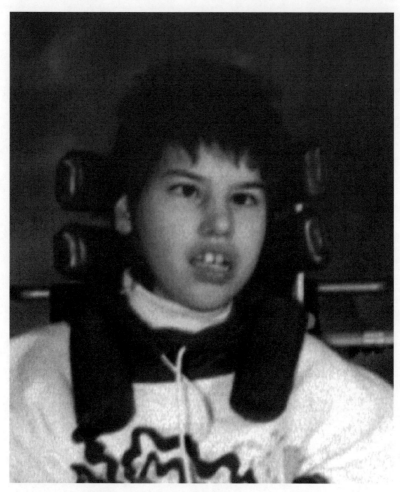

Tracy Latimer at about eleven years old.

Outside the courthouse, the Latimers wait for the verdict.

Robert Latimer's farm in Wilkie, Saskatchewan.

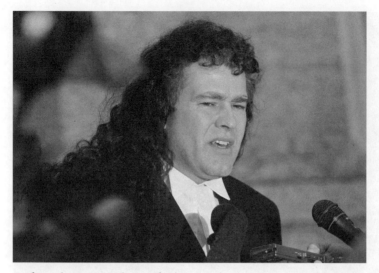

Defence lawyer Mark Brayford responds to reporters outside the Battleford courthouse, shortly after Robert Latimer was convicted of second-degree murder.

Miriam Edelson holds up a photo of herself and her severely disabled son Jake outside the Supreme Court of Canada in Ottawa in 2000. Miriam, who was in attendance for the Latimer case, believes that the courts should be lenient on Robert Latimer.

Protesters voice their support of Robert Latimer outside the Saskatchewan Provincial Correctional Institution in 2001.

Dave Clouston, deputy warden of William Head Prison, chats with media in Victoria about the release of Robert Latimer in 2008.

Robert Latimer talks with the media upon his arrival in Ottawa on March 17, 2008.

Robert Latimer shares a laugh with his sister, Marj Mosienko, upon his arrival in Ottawa.

CHAPTER 8
WORKING WITH ROBERT LATIMER

Robert Latimer is a man who committed an act of love and mercy that few others would have had the mental strength and determination to do. And he is a man who has been treated by the justice system in a cruel manner. This cruelty was not necessarily intentional, but rather a consequence of how the system works and a consequence of the influence of critics who thought that they, too, were doing the right thing. The justice system is not designed for cases like this, and Latimer himself is not designed for coping with a flawed justice system. He is a stubborn and inflexible man fighting against an unsympathetic and inflexible system that has been influenced at times by the voices of anti-euthanasia zealots. The result has been disastrous for him. One is tempted to say that the outcome was partly his own fault—except it is difficult to fault him for his own nature. His nature made him well suited to the life he led in rural Saskatchewan, where he wanted to be. He was just not well suited to deal with the legal maelstrom he found himself in.

Throughout all of my dealings with Robert Latimer he was almost always courteous, relaxed, and genial. Others found him this way, too. My observations in this chapter should not be read as portraying him as unfriendly. From the first time I met him in the canteen at William Head Prison in 2005, we had an easy and cordial relationship. I saw him frequently in prison between 2005 and 2008, when he was finally released on day parole, and then several times again when he moved back to Victoria from Ottawa in 2009. I live in Duncan, an hour's drive north of Victoria on Vancouver Island, and although his parole conditions normally prevented him from venturing more than twenty kilometres from his halfway house in downtown Victoria, he was able to get a pass one evening to come and visit my wife and me for dinner. He did not have transportation at the time so I picked him up and then drove him home before his curfew at 11 p.m. It was a very pleasant visit, and we talked about his time as a young man in the shipyards in Victoria. My wife and I both enjoyed his company that evening, as I had on many other occasions.

Still, it is part of the story that there is another side to the man, a side that allowed him to make a hard decision, but which did not stand him in good stead in coping with the consequences. I sometimes encountered his stubbornness, or perhaps it should be called his unshakable obstinacy, when it came to certain matters. He had been reasonably cooperative with me and was willing to give me some information about his situation, probably because I had helped him get his initial parole decision overturned. But I knew from the start that he was not comfortable with the idea of a book being written about him. He told me on several occasions that he had been asked many times if he would cooperate on writing a book and that he had refused. I think he was trying to steer me away.

He seemed comfortable enough with magazine articles and did not object to the first story I did on his situation, a short piece in autumn of 2006 in the magazine I was editing, *Humanist Perspectives*. The article was about the high regard we should have for acts of human compassion, in reaction to lobby groups, mostly representing certain religions, that maintain that human life must be protected at all costs. I wrote:

> *It is not mere human existence that we should hold sacred—it is human compassion. It is the willingness to help others, especially the most helpless among us, and the willingness to do so even at great personal cost, that we should accord the highest honour. And by that reckoning, Robert Latimer is a hero, not a murderer.*

Though he did not say much about it—the language was probably a bit overblown for him—he appreciated that I was trying to help him and that

I cared about him. And I avoided anything too personal. He spoke approvingly, too, of other supportive articles that had been written, particularly one by bioethicist and philosopher Alistair Brown. And he did not seem to mind a lengthy piece I wrote for *Humanist Perspectives* on his parole hearing in spring 2008, a piece that helped convince the BC Civil Liberties Association to launch the successful appeal. But the idea of a book struck him as more intrusive.

At first, Latimer talked quite openly with me, although he would back off whenever he thought I was getting too curious about his own feelings or about his family. There was always some underlying tension in our relationship, a tension that was due to the ambiguity of my role. Was I there to help him, or to get a story? Even I was not entirely sure about this. It was more of the former at first, then, after he was released from prison and my role progressed to that of author of this book, it became more of the latter.

Initially, I mostly had in mind trying to help, given the way he had been treated and the way some advocates of certain causes so viciously attacked him. I thought I could help best by writing articles in *Humanist Perspectives*, which was interested in exposing instances of social injustice. After we featured a story about the parole hearing, we published another on our counter-productive drug laws and policies, under the theme of "When the Law is an Ass," referring to the famous quote from Oliver Twist: "If the law supposes that," said Mr. Bumble, squeezing his hat emphatically in both hands, "the law is a ass—a idiot."

I thought that the law had been an ass in the Latimer case and that was a story worth telling, both to support Latimer and to raise public awareness of a serious injustice. Articles with limited intentions or purposes were fine with Latimer, and so long as I was operating within these boundaries (not that either one of us was thinking consciously about this, but both, I think, were intuitively aware of it) things were fine. I had no need of personal details.

When I told him I was going to expand my work into a book, however, things slowly started to change. Latimer would still talk to me about details—factual details—of his trials and various appeals and legal matters, but rarely would he say anything about his personal life. And he was unresponsive to my querying his views of the law or euthanasia, or anything other than a factual review of what had happened to him. He helped me quite a lot in working out an exact timeline for the complex series of legal events, and he did give me some interviews that I have drawn from and quoted in some places.

After I had completed a first draft of this book I asked if he would read it over, which he did. I did not hear back from him, so I phoned him and asked what he thought of it. "It seems fine," he said. I questioned him about some of the discussions later in the book, where I reflect on some larger issues, but he did not seem particularly interested. Later, when I mentioned that I was corresponding with a publisher about a manuscript on his case, he did not respond and changed the subject. I began to realize that he was becoming increasingly uncomfortable with the idea of a book.

Still, I was surprised when we came to the end of the line. As I was working on redrafts, I phoned him and said that, after discussions with the publisher, we decided we should have a few more details about his life. I added that I knew he was uncomfortable with this, but I wanted to be open with him and give him the opportunity to be the one to provide this information.

"I'm not too interested in that," he said.

"Could we meet for coffee somewhere and talk about it?" I asked.

"I don't like to talk about these things in public," he said, although he had done so in previous months. Still, this sounded hopeful. In spite of his reservations, I thought, it sounded like he would talk in the privacy of his apartment. He agreed to meet for lunch, which I supposed meant that we would go to his apartment for an interview afterwards. We met at a restaurant about a mile from his apartment. Wanting to honour his desire not to talk about his situation in public, I talked about other things, although I did throw in a few questions about farming in Saskatchewan, which he answered. But when I asked him about his father, he evaded the question. So I decided to wait on all such matters until we returned to his apartment. It was a congenial conversation, but superficial.

At the end of lunch he insisted on paying for both of us, something I had intended to do. I wondered why he did this, since I had asked him to lunch, and I worried a bit about its significance. I gave him a lift back to his apartment, and, as we were pulling into the driveway, he said: "About the book: we're really not interested in that." He paused, then added, "It's too intrusive." I immediately knew that my worries about his paying for lunch were well founded. This was not going to go as I had hoped. "We are not really interested in a book," he repeated.

"But," I said, "someone will write about your life, and it might as well be someone sympathetic."

"We aren't interested," he repeated. "We have had lots of requests before, but we aren't interested."

I wanted to say: "But you have been working with me. Why pull out now?" Or, "If I hadn't intervened, you'd still be in jail." Or something like that. But, happily, I did not. He had been through so much in the last fifteen years that he didn't owe me or anyone else anything. Still, this did not seem like a good decision on his part.

"What about your sisters?" I asked. "Do you not want me to talk to them?"

"They don't want to talk about this either," he said.

I did not think that was exactly true. I had previously talked extensively with his sister Marj Mosienko in Ottawa, and she, unlike her siblings, had talked publicly about Latimer's situation. I said nothing about that, though.

"You know," I said, "a lot of people regard you as a hero. They might want to read your story."

He laughed. "A lot of people don't, and I don't want to get them going again. As I say, we're just not interested."

"What if this scuttles the whole project?" I said, a bit hyperbolically. I was curious to see if he wanted the whole thing to go away, or just did not want to give out further personal information.

It was the former.

"You've still got the Martens book," he said, referring to another project he knew I was working on, about the prosecution of Evelyn Martens for assisted suicide. "I know you have put a lot of work into this, but we're just not interested."

There wasn't much more to say. I could sense that he had no intention of inviting me in to his apartment. This was it. We sat silently for a minute or two, then he got out, shook my hand, thanked me for what I had done, and said goodbye.

Initially, I was upset by this encounter. It meant we would no longer be working together on this book. But there was no real possibility that I would drop the project. I could get most of the information I needed from other sources. Latimer certainly had no obligation to help me any more than he already had, but whatever he felt about it, and whatever he had gone through for fifteen years, I was not going to stop my work. This was a story of interest and importance to many people, a story that should, in as much completeness as possible, be told.

Part of Latimer's resistance to having a book written about him is fear that publicity will hurt his family. He is a traditional father and husband who believes that it is his role to protect his wife and children. He believes that if the curiosity of millions of Canadians were indulged, it would disrupt their lives. In his view, family matters are private and nothing will persuade him otherwise. Furthermore, I suspect he is acutely uncomfortable talking about emotions at the best of times and would never reveal his feelings in public. As the Parole Board discovered, he would rather stay in jail.

Latimer is not interested in questions about euthanasia, inadequate laws as they pertain to euthanasia, or any other broader legal issues. He is not interested in how the law might be changed. He is not interested in the moral questions around it, either. He has little interest even in the matter of jury independence as it is related to his conviction in the first place. He is not a man of ideas; he is a man who sees the world in a practical way. He is someone who does what he sees has to be done.

Which brings us to the most difficult question of all. Was it wise for Latimer to take Tracy's fate into his own hands? I have no doubt, as I have indicated frequently in this book, that it was an act of mercy and compassion. It was also an act that required courage. And there is no question that Latimer should not have had to suffer in the way that he has. But for all of that, I cannot shake the feeling that he really ought not to have done it. It is a matter of relative harm. Tracy was undoubtedly better off dead, but she would likely have died soon anyway. Latimer could not bear to see her continued suffering, but in ending Tracy's life he seriously damaged his own life and that of the rest of his family. Was it worth it? It is impossible to say. I find myself both admiring his heroic act and questioning it, as well.

At some point I began to think of Latimer as having some of the characteristics of a tragic hero. He could have given the Parole Board what they wanted to hear, and been granted parole, by playing the game they clearly wanted him to play. Either he was not aware of how to do this, or would not do it, or both. Latimer at his parole hearing, like Shakespeare's Coriolanus, declined to display his wounds to the populace to gain public favour. Latimer is a self-sufficient, private, and practical man, qualities that served his life well at other times, and which allowed him to carry out a courageous compassionate act. But they were qualities that did not serve him so well in defending himself.

⁂

One of the more frustrating aspects of writing about the Latimer story is the elusiveness of Laura. The first time I met Latimer, at the William Head prison, I asked him how she was doing. I got a look from him that immediately told me that I hadn't yet learned the rules. We don't ask about her, and he doesn't say anything about her. So I backed off that topic, quickly.

Throughout the two more years he had at William Head, throughout the parole hearing, throughout his time on day parole, I never again asked him anything about his family. He would volunteer small bits of information, on occasion, but if I got too close to asking him anything about his family, I would see that look again.

Laura spoke at length at the trial, and after the Supreme Court hearing she gave full interviews to CBC and CTV News. But soon afterwards she began to think that the publicity was hurting the children and for the most part she stopped talking publicly. Both she and Robert worked hard at helping their children through this ordeal. They kept them fully informed, and whenever any major event was about to come up, perhaps where the children's names would be mentioned on television, they would warn the children and also go to the children's school and speak to the teachers, who in turn would talk to the other school children about what was happening to Robert. In this way the Latimer children seem to have been spared the schoolyard taunting that often occurs in such situations.

One misleading suggestion that is sometimes made about Laura in the writings of Latimer's most extreme critics is that she intended at first to testify for the prosecution, but then thought better of it and testified for the defence. The implication is that she disagreed with what her husband

115

did and wanted to see him punished for it, but then relented at the last moment. These critics don't say exactly that, but they leave readers who are already hostile to the Latimers with the impression that something like that occurred. This is the sort of thing that often happens to the Latimers. It makes their reluctance to talk understandable.

The critics who make this suggestion about Laura are either dishonestly or ignorantly interpreting a couple of events and coming to an entirely unsupportable contention. Laura was, according to her own testimony, angry when she first found out what her husband had done; not, as critics suggest, because she thought Tracy should live, but because he had got himself into so much trouble. Her anger lasted for a few days until she was finally allowed to speak to him, and then she accepted that what he had done was right. At one point the prosecution was going to call her as a witness—a hostile one. But when Brayford said he intended to put her on the stand as a defence witness, Neufeld no longer needed to call her, so he dropped her from his list. Neufeld wanted to go after her with her diary, but he could only do so in cross-examination. Laura was and always has been intensely loyal to her husband.

Though it is difficult to extract a detailed profile of Laura, given the position she and Robert share in regard to personal information, we can get a bit of a sense of her from the public comments she has made, some of which are reported below.

After her husband was convicted for the first time on November 16, 1994, she sobbed outside the Battleford courthouse and said, "Whatever hell they put him through will not begin to match the hell that our little girl went through." She wondered how the justice system could lock up a "good and loving" father who had been so devoted to Tracy.

After the 1997 conviction she had indicated that she would not answer questions, but then she responded angrily to a question about how they were going to manage the farm. "Bob might go to jail. The farm is the last thing on our minds. I'm more worried about my husband than the stupid farm."

When Latimer was sent to prison on January 18, 2001, a reporter asked her how she felt about the fact that her husband had been sent to a maximum-security prison, instead of the low- or medium-security prison they had hoped for. She answered, "I thought my heart couldn't break anymore. But I found out I was wrong, I'm extremely upset."

During Laura's CBC and CTV television interviews, a little over a week after the Supreme Court decision, she spoke highly of her husband, saying, "Bob phoned me from jail. And he just kind of poured strength out to me over the phone. And it amazed me. How can you be in jail, facing a lifetime sentence, and pour strength out to the family?" She went on to say that they were a "close family. I don't know if all of this has brought us closer or not, but we are, and you know, Bob phones us every day from jail. He talks to the kids every day. He's still parenting them from jail…I guess I just want people to know…this is a real family, there's real kids here, there's a real dad, you know, who can't come home for ten years. This is a real family. It's not some abstract issue."

In the weeks following his imprisonment, Laura attended candlelight vigils on her husband's behalf, one outside the walls of the Saskatchewan Penitentiary, where Latimer had been sent. She wept as she spoke to a crowd of about three hundred supporters. "People are writing, they're wearing ribbons, they're signing petitions, it's really fantastic," she said. "We love you, Bob, we want you home, we miss you…We're going to keep watching, we're not going to rest, we won't rest until you're home."

When her husband was denied parole in December of 2007 she was approached by the media and said, "It's just a sad day, that's all. Really sad." She had not attended the hearing because, she claimed, she wanted to avoid the media. She reiterated that she had decided not to talk to the media about herself or her husband's situation, because "It just sort of turns into a circus."

Laura was contacted by the press immediately after it was announced that her husband had been granted day parole in February 2008. "I am just so excited," she said. "My son just came home so I want to talk to him. I just told him two seconds ago. He's just thrilled. It's wonderful. This will be food for all of our souls." When asked why her husband was going to Ottawa on day parole she said, "He does have his reasons, but you'll have to ask him that." She added that she expected him to return to the farm in three years when his day parole, and the requirement to stay in a halfway house, ended.

Some have characterized Latimer's lone action as that of an alpha male or father-knows-best type, and Laura's steadfast support as that of a traditional, obedient wife. But this does not seem to capture their relationship. Laura was certainly loyal to her husband, but he was loyal to her as well. He acted alone, but his action in ending Tracy's life was based upon his knowledge that she, too, thought it would be for the best. There may have been an element of "a man doing what he's got to do," and the good woman supporting him, but there are ambiguities in every aspect of this case. And Latimer's solitary decision also protected Laura from prosecution. It seems to me that Robert and Laura have been in this together, in spirit, in a mutually supportive way, from the time Tracy was born to the day she died, and then afterwards through all of their tribulations. To denigrate the loyalty they have shown each other seems churlish and mean spirited.

There are many examples of people characterizing both Robert and Laura Latimer in exaggerated ways. Robert in particular has been unmercifully pilloried in some quarters, in a way that entirely fails to understand the man and the dilemma that he truly believed he faced.

But calling the Latimers either villains or heroes misses the mark. Looking at the whole sorry sequence of events, it is difficult not to be moved by the Latimers' plight, by their efforts to cope, and by the underlying human decency they evidently possess. These are good people who faced misfortune of the sort that could happen to any of us. It is neither vilification nor adoration that they deserve; it is sympathy and human understanding.

CHAPTER 9
LATIMER'S CRITICS

Although all the evidence presented in the trials strongly indicates that Latimer was motivated by love and mercy, certain critics have frequently accused him, often with extraordinary hostility, of having other motivations. Why such anger, why such certainty, why such determination to punish a man who, any reasoned examination of the case must allow, at least *might* have been engaged in a merciful act, at considerable personal risk? How can such a possibility be so determinedly excluded? How is it that the panel members at Latimer's parole hearing went after him with such strange aggression, which was still mild compared to some of the public comments that have been made about him?

The hostility is much more than a concern about there being, as Speck said, "all sorts of people who hold moral views that say we'd all be better off if we could go and kill a lot of people," an inelegant expression of a legitimate social concern about people's making their own decisions about taking another's life. That indeed is a legitimate concern, and there must be legal safeguards against irresponsible acts of assisted suicide and euthanasia. But in the absence of controlled, legally sanctioned procedures for certain problematic end-of-life situations there will be circumstances where desperate people take desperate actions; merciful, but illegal actions. Robert Latimer was a desperate person who resorted to a desperate action.

It might be necessary to prosecute someone like Latimer, to make a statement about the unacceptability of taking the life of another person, but surely such a prosecution, and the resulting public commentary, should be tempered with at least a hint of mercy, a suggestion of understanding, a modicum of human sympathy. Indiscriminate and venomous attacks upon anyone involved in assisted suicide and euthanasia fail to allow for the possibility that these individuals acted for merciful reasons, not malicious ones. Someone who ends the desperate suffering of any other animal is seen as performing a difficult act of kindness. Someone who does the same for a human being is called a murderer and denounced, by some, with utter contempt.

Why this angry wind? Why the personal attacks, the misrepresentation of evidence, the denial of even the possibility that what these people do can be construed as an act of mercy? Why the aggression that goes far beyond the reasonable position that, given the law as it stands, some sort of prosecution may be necessary? In the Latimer case, a response has been triggered that is clearly irrational and unbalanced.

The Latimer case has had much press coverage over a long period of time, and the nature of his action—non-voluntary euthanasia—is inherently difficult and controversial; I am not denying that. But the ongoing campaign of strong and unsympathetic denunciation seems very out of balance. This negative position was exemplified by the comments made in the media scrum following the Parole Board hearing, in comments made by Rory Summers, president of the BC Association of Community Living, and by Laney Bryenton, executive director of the same organization. These self-described "advocates for the disabled" were observers at the hearing, and spoke to reporters after the decision to refuse parole was announced.

As I approached the cluster of reporters, I heard Summers and Bryenton talking about one particular question put to Latimer in the hearing. Kelly-Ann Speck had asked Latimer if he had found it difficult to accept Tracy after the brain damage had occurred. He had replied by saying something about it being a tragedy. Summers exclaimed that *"He* [Latimer] *even called her birth a tragedy!"* suggesting, as the board had, that this was a callous and unfeeling man. But of course Latimer had been referring to the injury Tracy had sustained at birth, an injury that deprived her of any semblance of a normal life. That, by any rational accounting, was indeed a tragedy.

Summers and Bryenton went on to make several other statements: "We were very pleased with the outcome [the denial of parole]. We heard absolutely no remorse."

"We were disturbed by his complete lack of remorse for the murder of his daughter."

"Part of parole is admitting what you did was wrong, and he did not."

(Summers and Bryenton were apparently unaware that remorse is not considered a suitable consideration in the granting of parole. Nor did they appear to have any understanding of the unsuitability of remorse as an emotion for someone to feel after carrying out an act of mercy.)

Summers and Bryenton went on to say: "As a parent, when you have a child, you cherish that child."

I came across no one—not a family member, not a friend, not a doctor, not anyone who actually knew Robert Latimer—who thought that he did not love his daughter. There was no indication that his jury, or his trial judge, or his appeal judges, or the Supreme Court justices, or even his prosecutor doubted that he loved his daughter. Summers and Bryenton, two people who did not know Robert Latimer, after watching his uncomfortable and unfair interrogation by the Parole Board, apparently had no compunctions about suggesting that he did not love his daughter.

"We represent people at risk and people without a voice. Tracy has no voice now. Her voice has been silenced. We are representing Tracy."

In fact, Tracy never had a voice. But if we were to suppose she could express her wishes, one wonders whom she would want representing her interests—her parents, who had loved her and cared for her, attentively and with great concern for her welfare, for twelve years, or people who appeared to be using her to advance the political agenda of their organization.

They added: "He wants to go to Ottawa to advocate for his position."

This comment appeared to reflect a concern that if Latimer got out of prison, he would become an advocate for euthanasia. But Latimer was not proposing to go to Ottawa for that purpose; he is not and probably never will be an advocate of legalized euthanasia. He wanted to go there in part to seek certain answers about what he believes were errors in the evidence presented by the prosecution in his case.

"He thinks what he did was right! We don't think he was right! He murdered his daughter!"

As Alan Borovoy, the head of the Canadian Civil Liberties Association, said when interviewed after seeing video clips of the Summers-Bryenton comments, it is wrong to classify all deaths at another's hand as the same; to say that all are murders. There are cases, he said, like Latimer's, where there are extreme extenuating circumstances, and the law should make special provision for such cases. Summers and Bryenton, however, apparently consider those caught in terrible moral dilemmas, as Robert Latimer was, to be the same as any other "murderers."

"The man showed no emotion. He couldn't even remember the date she died," Summers said.

This sort of comment was like the questionable character analysis attempted by the Parole Board members. Some people hide their emotions, especially a private man like Robert Latimer. Not displaying any emotion is different from not feeling any emotion. Neither Kelly-Ann Speck nor the duo of Summers and Bryenton (likely taking their cue from Speck's aggressive and unfair questioning on this subject) were in a position to make such claims. As discussed before, Latimer is clearly most uncomfortable with discussing matters he considers to be personal, and being forced to do so with the world watching (through the eyes of reporters) must have been very difficult for him. No one knows what emotions were running through his mind, but we can be sure that he would be most guarded about revealing them.

And let me add a personal comment of my own regarding the date that Tracy died. My own daughter died several years ago, in quite different but difficult circumstances. I cannot bear to think about the date, because of the grief that would hit me every year when that day came by. I have blocked it out and, if asked, I would not be able to give the date. This is one way in which I cope with my intense feelings about her death. Ways of coping with grief are individual and cannot be prescribed.

Summers said that he himself has a son who is disabled and who, like Tracy, had rods inserted in his body to keep it more rigid. This is the operation often done to relieve scoliosis, and it usually does help the patient in certain ways, like allowing him or her to breathe more easily and to sit in a chair. These improvements indeed happened for Tracy, but, as even her orthopaedic surgeon admitted, the overall effect was a decline in Tracy's already marginal quality of life.

Why would Summers add this comment about his own son? The clear implication was that he, Summers, had been in a position similar to that of Latimer. Such comments are frequently made by people who have a child with a disability of some kind. But the analogies are mostly false ones. Summers's son was not like Tracy. For one thing, Summers inadvertently illustrated this point by stating that his son thanked him for the operation. Tracy could not even understand that she had had an operation, much less thank anyone for it—or speak at all. And her escalating pain in the year following her back operation, and the prospect of more severe surgery on her tiny, exhausted body were the things Latimer faced. Despite his implication that he had done so, Summers had not walked in Latimer's shoes.

❦

Latimer's critics are troubling in the way that they simplistically denounce actions of considerable moral complexity. More important, they often seem to be pursuing goals that are essentially ideological, and in doing so they misrepresent evidence and mislead the public, making rational public discussion and sensible public policy more difficult to achieve.

The arguments put forward by the anti-euthanasia lobbyists seem to be based upon two underlying concerns: an unwavering disapproval (except in the cases of war or capital punishment) of human-induced death of any sort; and an entrenched conviction that the intentional ending of the life of any disabled person will release the murderous dogs upon all the disabled.

These concerns are not immoral ones. They are based upon particular understandings of moral responsibilities. Still, the consequence of both is not a more caring society, but one that is too afraid to make rational and compassionate decisions about end-of-life matters. The anti-euthanasia lobbyists, the more extreme ones at least, try to block calm and sensible discussion about how we ought to handle situations where, for example, a desperately ill and dying person wants to die. Those interested in helping people even in such seemingly obvious cases are described in scathing terms by the extremists, who frequently engage in emotional behaviours designed to disrupt attempts at rational discussion. A severely disabled and apparently ill person was wheeled into the courtroom for Laura Latimer's testimony and proceeded to cough and make sounds that frequently distracted the jury and the other participants in the trial.

In working toward a more just society, we often must look past the some-times alarming rhetoric of extremists to carefully and rationally address the issues, seeking solutions that are wise and compassionate. End-of-life issues arise in the lives of all of us, for ourselves and for all the friends and relatives who predecease us. We need to ensure that our laws and public policies on these matters are not skewed by voices of unreason.

It might be helpful to examine and to try to understand these voices; because, if we persist in allowing them to influence our public business, there is little hope that, in regard to end-of-life issues and many other issues of human importance, we will evolve toward a more just and com-passionate society.

~~❀~~

The Nazi regime in Germany in the mid-twentieth century was a horrifying-ly repugnant one, so much so that any activity that conjures up the image of Nazi atrocities is immediately and often justifiably tainted. The Nazis' idea of building a master race by using the so-called science of eugenics and by euthanizing "undesirables" has left a terrible and still-unhealed wound in modern consciousness. That such a thing could have happened and could have been carried out by ordinary human beings is indeed why we must be forever vigilant in regard to further expressions of the forces of unreason that release the darkest human impulses.

But the battle against unreason is not won by more unreason; not by a "triumph of the will." It is won, to the extent it can be won, by the firm and determined application of reason mixed with human compassion.

Some continue to argue today that because euthanasia was used in such an egregious manner by the Nazis, we must never again allow euthanasia in any form whatsoever. There are various societies and associations devoted to attempting to ensure that all varieties of euthanasia (in this discussion I am using euthanasia in the broadest sense, meaning it to include assisted suicide) remain forever banned. But is this a rational response to what the Nazis did?

Perhaps the best way of illustrating the fallacy here is to draw an analogy. The Nazis used public education as a means of indoctrinating the young. Many other unsavoury regimes have also done so. Shall we ban public education, then, to prevent it from becoming a tool for indoctrination by authorities? Of course we would not do that; instead we work to find ways of preventing malign indoctrination from happening, knowing that the potential for abuse doesn't negate the importance of public education. As a civilized society, as a democracy, we must have education for all. Of that there can be little doubt.

What then of euthanasia? Is it just a tool for eugenics? It even sounds like eugenics. Is it not just a way to legalize the culling of inferior people? The analogy with public education breaks down, some will argue, because public education has a very valuable side to it, while euthanasia does not.

But ask those dying in agony, those who have no hope of anything that will significantly ease the terrible burden, for them, of ongoing life. Ask those who live in fear of declining into a vegetative state, perhaps kept alive by drastic medical interventions, who find the idea of such an existence abhorrent? Ask those who wish to die when they become fully disabled, but know that then they would be incapable of doing anything about it themselves. Such people, and they could be any of us, and almost surely will include someone we know, will not say that euthanasia is unimport-ant. They, or most of them, will tell you that it is of central importance to their lives, more important than almost anything else to them at that time, even more than the idea of public education.

Euthanasia imposed by the state, in the service of eugenics, is unaccept-able. But euthanasia allowed by the state, to relieve hideous suffering, is an act of mercy. State-imposed euthanasia denies the most basic of human rights, the right to live. But state-supported euthanasia is a validation of personal autonomy, which means not only the right to live but also the right to die.

This distinction between different ideas about euthanasia is critical—the one being a denial of freedom and justice, the other being a confirmation of the right to personal freedom. The one is state-imposed abuse, the ultimate denial of personal autonomy; the other (when properly constituted) is state-regulated to prevent abuse and confirm personal autonomy. It is like a (hypo-thetical) system of state-enforced abortions, serving a government program of eugenics, as opposed to a state-supported program of allowing abortions for women who want them.

Some argue that even though a rational distinction between approaches to euthanasia is possible, introducing it at all is venturing onto a slippery slope. We need to step back, take a deep breath, and examine this argument. Is all that is stopping a despicable program of state-enforced eugenics in Canada the fact that we do not allow euthanasia under any circumstances? We make all sorts of public policy decisions which, if abused or taken to an extreme, would lead to bad consequences, yet in a civilized and just society we must continue to make policy decisions. We need regulations to prevent abuse, not prohibition.

❦

Some people of certain religious faiths believe that human lives should not be taken under any circumstances: as some put it, human life is a sacred journey and only God can decide when it should be ended. For such people the taking of any human life is reprehensible. The mercy killing of a person in desperate, intractable pain is just as bad as, say, serial murder. In a free society the views of such people must be accepted, insofar as their own lives are concerned. But is it right that such views, held by a small minority of people, be imposed on all of society?

A minority view can of course be a morally superior one, and that is what the religious opponents of euthanasia claim. Even if few agree, they will say, we are obliged to fight for what is right. But do they have a strong case for being "right"? If they did, then all of us would have a moral obligation to listen to them. They cannot be dismissed simply because they are in a small minority.

Let us look at this belief in the need to defer to what is perceived to be the will of God. One problem with this religious perspective on death is that it is contrary to a belief in personal autonomy, a belief that (among other things) holds that we ought to have the right to make decisions about our own bodies. Why should we choose one belief over another? One reason that a rational person might choose belief in personal autonomy is that it is based upon the ideas of personal dignity and freedom and upon respect for human individuality. Declaring the primacy of God's will, on the other hand, is fraught with arbitrariness and inconsistencies, since different groups and faiths have quite different ideas about just what God's will happens to be. When there are many different interpretations by people of faith, how can one particular view, no matter how strongly believed, be the basis of public policy?

Moreover, there are some serious inconsistencies in the position of many religious people regarding interference in God's plan for us. There are rarely any objections from them to increasing our natural life span through medical intervention, which would seem to be as much an interference of God's plan as is the ending of a life of suffering. It would be a strange God who would condone what amounts to prolonging an agonizing dying process, which is what often happens when extraordinary measures are used to keep a person technically alive, but forbids the merciful shortening of terrible suffering.

Furthermore, many people who object to the premature ending of a life in pain, of someone who wants to die, are not pacifists: they do not object in general to wars in which people who want to live are purposefully killed. And many also support capital punishment. The Christian Right in North America is well known for holding these contradictory views, though some other opponents of euthanasia are more consistent in this regard.

The opposition to human intervention in the ending of life (except for those "acceptable" killings mentioned above) usually comes from those who believe that the moment of conception is something engineered by God and that the newly fertilized egg has sacred status, and must be given all of the rights and privileges (insofar as that is possible) of a fully-formed human being. In opposing contraception, the Pope has said that it "is a means of negating the intimate truth of conjugal love, with which the divine gift [of life] is communicated." Such a divine gift cannot be subjected to mortal control.

If one really believes in such a notion of life then the opposition to both abortion and self-chosen death makes sense. But does such a belief itself make sense? Unfortunately, religious beliefs do not have to make sense, and often do not. Religious beliefs are handed down as matters of faith and are not based upon evidence or reason. That does not mean they are wrong (though most must be wrong in some sense, because different religious beliefs are inconsistent with one another), nor does it mean that people should be denied their beliefs. It does, though, argue for the importance of secular laws that will disallow any particular faith from having dominion over another, or over those of no religious faith.

One more point should be made about the religious opposition to euthanasia and assisted suicide. This opposition is sometimes called the "moral" or "principled" position on end-of-life issues. But this claiming of the moral high ground is misleading. The religious view described above, representing an unnuanced opposition to the ending of human life, is based upon simplistic and arbitrary interpretations of ancient scriptures; arbitrary in that particular passages of scripture have been given precedence over others. This selectivity leads to arbitrary and absolute rules, which are highly debatable even if one grants religious authority to these scriptures. Why should such an approach be ceded the moral high ground? What about those who, instead, base their sense of morality on a compassionate consideration of the interests of the people involved?

❧

Appearing as interveners in Latimer's last Supreme Court hearing, on June 14, 2000, were representatives of two religious groups and a spokesperson for a coalition of groups who feel that Latimer, by his actions, and indeed all those who support the right-to-die movement and similar movements, threaten the disabled; or, as they sometimes more emotively put it, "the fragile among us." They claim that permitting the taking of any life "will lead to open season on the disabled."

This well-intended perspective is partly a consequence of reaction against Nazi policies and against other exercises in eugenics, such as the forced sterilization programs for certain handicapped groups that were carried out in Alberta in the 1950s. The idea of eugenics had a certain logical appeal at the time; for example, it is clearly problematic for a woman with a severe mental handicap to have a child. But where to draw the line? For euthanasia and assisted suicide, sensible lines can be drawn; for one thing, they can be based upon unbiased assessments of clear, unequivocal, and unforced expressions of the wishes of the person in question. Such a restriction would essentially eliminate the possibility of abuse (though it would not cover rare cases like that of Tracy Latimer). In the case of forced sterilization, however, sensible and safe standards and controls are much more difficult to formulate, and I agree with those who argue against any such sort of program as dangerous and unwise.

Many of those who see themselves as defenders of the disabled have a connection themselves with a disabled person, whom they love and care for. And it is laudable that they do so, and that they fight for better support and care for the weak and needy. In this they deserve the strongest possible support.

But some advocates for the disabled entirely misread the objectives of right-to-die movements, which are also based on love and caring. These movements have nothing to do with culling out supposedly inferior humans, as the fear seems to be. They are about the very opposite of human cruelty; they are about protecting, not abusing, individual human rights. They are about living in freedom and, if one so chooses, having the freedom to die as one wishes to die. They are not about disrespecting human life, as some advocates for the disabled mistakenly claim; they are about respecting individual freedom and the dignity of human life.

Some critics of Latimer's action take the position that, because Tracy had no choice in the matter, her fundamental human right to life was violated. This concern highlights the problematic nature of non-voluntary euthanasia, where there can be no consent, as compared to assisted suicide or voluntary euthanasia, where there is consent. And it must be conceded that non-voluntary euthanasia is a much more difficult issue. But the philosophy behind all right-to-die movements is the same: to protect one's right of personal autonomy. People ought to have the right to control what happens to their own bodies and have the right to die in circumstances of their choosing, with help if necessary. Non-voluntary euthanasia is an extension of this idea, for those incapacitated to the point where they are not able to express their wishes. It is based upon an assessment of what such a person could reasonably be thought to have wanted, but was unable to express. Ideally this would come from some prior statement by the person, although in cases like that of Tracy Latimer this would not be possible. Human decency, though, would seem to require that, in such cases, it should somehow be made a legal option; not through an individual decision but through a carefully controlled legal process.

Like religious opponents of assisted suicide and euthanasia, many supporters of the disabled make no distinction at all between assisted suicide and euthanasia, even non-voluntary euthanasia, and make no allowance for mitigating circumstances. Consent to have assistance in dying makes no difference at all; it is the dying that is considered wrong. According to this view, all such actions are equally bad, so the distinctions between assisted suicide, at one end of the spectrum of moral complexity, and non-voluntary euthanasia, at the other, make no real difference. Such people will use the potential horrors of eugenics to bolster their cause, but essentially they see little moral difference between eugenics and, say, helping a miserable dying person to escape from his or her personal horror.

The spokesperson for the coalition of groups representing the interests of the disabled at Latimer's Canadian Supreme Court hearing argued that Latimer's act was an attack on the disabled. He rejected Latimer's argument that Tracy's life was ended because of pain by arguing that her pain was the result of her disability and, therefore, her life was ended because she was disabled. This is grossly unfair to the Latimers, who had been dedicated to doing whatever they could to help Tracy for twelve years; they fully accepted her as she was and were devoted to her. But the reasoning is not only unfair, it is specious. The claim is that because the source of her pain was her disability, therefore her life was ended because of her disability, and killing someone because of a disability is wrong. But this is like arguing that it would be wrong to help someone in intense terminal pain to die because the pain was the result of cancer, and it is wrong to end the life of a person just because they have cancer. Of course the source of the agony in both cases was the affliction, but the affliction itself was not the reason for death. Tracy lived for over twelve years with her terrible condition; it was only when the pain became too intense, too difficult to mitigate, too certain to get worse, that Latimer took action. The point was the pain and deterioration of life, not the source of the pain. Latimer did not end Tracy's life because she had afflictions; he did so because the pain caused by her afflictions had become, in Latimer's view, unbearable. It is one thing to think that we cannot, as a society, permit individual decisions in such matters. It is another to severely punish and condemn an act of mercy.

There is no suggestion in any testimony that Latimer thought Tracy should die because of her severe disability. He never indicated that he thought Tracy was "unworthy" of life, as some in the disabled lobby claim; he thought instead that her life no longer was worth living, not because she was an unworthy person, but because of her pain.

One of the oddest arguments used against Latimer in his various trials and appeals, reiterated by the spokesperson for the coalition of supporters of the disabled in Latimer's final Supreme Court appeal hearing, was that pain is a subjective thing and some feel it more than others. Maybe Tracy's apparent pain was not so bad. This seems like arguments once used to justify operations on babies without using anesthetics; the view seemed to be then that unarticulated pain was not pain to worry about. Like those babies, all Tracy could do was cry out when she felt pain; she could not, for example, measure it on a scale of one to ten, as caregivers like to ask patients to do. She could not even understand the words of such a question, or any question, let alone give an intelligible response. So maybe, the argument seemed to be, her pain was not as bad as, say, that of a normal person who underwent such traumas. But in her uncomprehending state, maybe it was worse. There is no way to know. Maybe a life of minimal awareness marked by episodes of what to most people would be excruciating pain is even more terrible, more terrifying. The Latimers, in twelve years of very close observation of Tracy, were likely the best judges of her pain. To attempt to undermine the Latimer defence by suggesting that Tracy's pain might not have been all that bad seems to dehumanize her, or not take her humanity fully into account. And this accusation, which we can level against Latimer's critics, is the same one they have used against him.

❧

Entangled in all of the above is the "slippery slope" argument. It goes like this: If you permit any legalized interference with the continued life of any person, no matter what sort of hopeless distress they are in, then what is to stop the taking of other lives in less distress, or even those who might simply fall short of some arbitrary definition of human perfection?

It is important to separate this argument from the religious one about the sacredness of human life. If we are still bothered about the idea that any human life is ever ended on any account, we will find it difficult to make a clear-headed assessment of the slippery slope argument. If our premise is a religious one that prohibits the taking of a life in any circumstance, then there is no need to argue about slippery slopes because the taking of more lives, as imagined in the slippery slope argument, is not the point. In the religious view, it is the taking of a life *per se* that is indefensible. So by separating the two we can better assess the validity of each. If neither is valid on its own then the two conflated will be equally invalid. Two unreasonable arguments cannot make a reasonable one.

Is the slippery slope argument reasonable? Concern about slippery slopes is legitimate in some cases. Anyone who has ever tried a diet knows that it is often easier to abstain completely from certain fattening foods, because taking one bite blurs the line between abstinence and consumption, and the next bite and each bite after that are much easier. This is a well-known and real psychological phenomenon, one that is all the more problematic in cases of alcohol and drug addiction. A similar sort of process exists in many other aspects of life, some relatively trivial, others less so. Once one has committed a theft or a murder, it may be easier to do so again.

But in most cases where a slippery slope is a legitimate concern, it is a matter of stepping onto a slope that leads to gratifying some harmful or undesirable personal urge. Taking an action that has no element of harmful personal gratification— ay, putting oneself at risk by rescuing a person from drowning—has no slippery slope consequence. If doing such a thing once makes it easier to do another time, then fine: it really makes no sense to think of someone being on a slippery slope to hell for committing, for example, an act of mercy.

The idea of a slippery slope is that we slide into doing things we ought not to do. Acts of kindness and selflessness are not such things.

Now what is the case with ending or helping to end another person's life? In many instances such actions truly are murder and are carried out for self-serving and unacceptable reasons, such as jealousy, greed, or hatred. The Nazis were motivated by their hatred of Jews, self-aggrandizing delusions, and desire for political gain. Whatever the motivation, it was nothing good, kind, or generous. As mentioned earlier, there is a slippery slope problem with murder, and presumably with any real crime. So, aside from dealing with the injustice in the first place, and setting suitable punishment for the act itself, it is important to take punitive action in order to prevent a person from murdering again. It is in such cases that the slippery slope argument has traction, and it can be an effective political tactic, then, to extrapolate to other situations where the analogy might appear on the surface to be apt, but upon examination is not.

Clearly, the ending of a life out of mercy is something different from murder. We make this distinction all the time in the animal world, where the cruel mistreatment of any animal is a criminal offence, but the mercy killing of an animal is regarded as an act of kindness. And in such instances we are not worried about those who take the life of the animal as likely to go on a spree of wantonly killing animals that are in less difficult circumstances. Yet that is exactly what opponents of mercy killing of humans want to claim. Can we really believe that taking the life of a severely distressed and wretched person with no possibility of a decent life, a person who has not and never will again have any desire to keep living, will lead to the killing of others who might want to live?

If, then, we can establish that the ending of a life was a truly merciful act, as all real evidence in the Latimer case suggests, then the notion of a slippery slope in such a case makes no sense. Where would the slippery slope be taking us—to more merciful acts? This is not to say that we can be sanguine about attributions of mercy. The taking of a life must always be subject to careful scrutiny. It would be best if euthanasia were sanctioned by law, so that it could be carefully regulated and controlled.

But what of the effect of allowing such things to be sanctioned by laws; what of the "culture of death" that would supposedly create? This is a version of the slippery slope: that we would descend into a society that does not value life and that callously ends life whenever it is convenient to do so. But how can we imagine that acts of kindness might lead to a culture of death? How would that work? How does respecting personal autonomy translate to a loss of respect for human life? How would allowing people to make decisions about their own bodies lead to a lack of respect for other human's bodies?

In the interests of open-mindedness and without evidence to the contrary, we would have to allow that the dire prophecies about a culture of death descending on society, as absurd as they seem, could somehow come true. But, fortunately, even that obscure possibility can be dismissed by the evidence. In jurisdictions where assisted suicide and/or euthanasia legislation has been passed, no such thing has happened. In Oregon—the one North American jurisdiction where physician-aided suicide has been legal for some years—there has been no sudden rash of suicides, no culture of death, and only a very limited number of terminally-ill people who have actually taken advantage of this enlightened law. The law was enacted in 1997 and in the first ten years fewer than fifty people each year actually ended their lives with the lethal medication prescribed for them that year. Many others have obtained the medications but not yet used them, but rest more easily knowing that if their condition worsens they have that option easily open. This is civility and human kindness, not a culture of death.

CHAPTER 10
HOW LATIMER WAS
DENIED JUSTICE

What are we to do when a serious injustice appears to be the result of application of the law; in particular, when criminality is attributed to non-criminals? What means can we use to permit a sense of human decency to intervene in such instances, without undermining the law and respect for the law?

Most people, no matter what they feel about the Latimer case, can imagine a circumstance in which they would be very uncomfortable with a strict application of the law; a circumstance where a person is technically guilty of a crime, but really ought not to be punished for it. Do we simply accept such punishment as collateral damage necessary to maintain law and order? Do we sacrifice unfortunate individuals to uphold the sanctity of the law? Or do we have a mechanism allowing for consideration of extenuating circumstances even when the law says there are none?

We do have such a mechanism. We have juries of peers designated to make the final decision on questions of guilt or innocence. Juries are carefully informed about the law by the judge during the process of the trial and are encouraged by the courts to respect the law. But juries are independent entities, however much judges may try to hide that fact. Juries are entirely free to make decisions contrary to a literal reading of the law, contrary to legal precedents, contrary to the instructions given by the presiding judge, contrary even to an uncoerced and unquestioned admission of guilt. They are free to render the verdict they feel they ought to render, whatever the facts and the law happen to be. And if they make a decision contrary to law, they are not required to justify or to explain their decision (they are not even allowed to do so, in Canada). Such a jury decision, contrary to law, is called "jury nullification" of the law. It is sometimes referred to as the doctrine of jury independence.

This process is the one legitimate way the law can be overridden; it is the one way that the community can step in and say that the application of the law in a particular case is unjust, without thereby sanctioning casual law-breaking. Though rare in practice, and actively discouraged by the judiciary, it is a right that all juries in Canada (and in Britain and the United States) have.

One would think, however, on hearing what the judiciary has to say about it, that there is something almost evil about jury nullification. The Supreme Court has a very low opinion of it, and judges in Canada generally do everything possible to avoid it. In one extreme case, Grant Krieger was convicted on December 3, 2003, for growing and selling marijuana. He had been approved to do so for his own medical condition, multiple sclerosis, but had been selling it to others who were also using it for medical purposes. This was a case where, though technically guilty, the defendant would likely have had much sympathy from the jury. The trial judge, Justice Paul Chrumka, undoubtedly concerned about the possibility of nullification, made an extraordinary statement to the jury, telling them to: "…retire to the jury room to consider what I have said, appoint one of yourselves to be your foreperson, and then return to the court with a verdict of guilty."

When troubled jurors subsequently questioned Justice Chrumka on his direction to them, he told them unequivocally that they must return a verdict of guilty, which they ultimately did. Although it seemed likely that this decision would be turned over on appeal, it was not, at first. The Alberta Court of Appeal rejected the appeal, in spite of a strong and articulate dissent by Alberta Chief Justice Catherine Fraser. Eventually, three years after the initial conviction, the Supreme Court of Canada did support the appeal and overturned the verdict on the grounds that a directed verdict of guilty is not permissible. A trial judge does have the power, in effect, to direct a verdict of not guilty by dismissing a case, but he does not have the power to direct a verdict of guilty. A judge cannot, and should not, be allowed to override a jury's inherent right to find a defendant not guilty.

While the Supreme Court decision was an obvious one in this case—some have described it as the most expected decision in the history of the Court—one is left to wonder, not only about Justice Chrumka, and the astonishing arrogance and presumptiveness of his instruction to the jury, but also about the two Alberta appeal judges who disagreed with Chief Justice Fraser in the initial appeal.

In this case, at least, the Supreme Court came out on the side of jury independence—that criminality is to be decided by jurors and not directed by judges. As we shall see, however, the Court's concession in this extreme instance did not reflect a more general acceptance of the idea of jury independence.

❧

A basic civil liberty in our society is the right to the best possible defence in a criminal trial. This is central to the administration of justice, giving necessary protection to prosecuted individuals against the power of the state. Although the best defence is limited at times by practical considerations, such as the cost of hiring the best lawyers and the inadequacy of legal aid, it is still a foundational point in our justice system.

Jury nullification represents one important way, in certain kinds of cases, of providing for this basic civil liberty. In Latimer's case, it was very clear that his best defence—really his only defence—was that what he did was not murder, not an act of malice, and that the charge of murder—while fitting the law as it is written—was unsuitable in this instance. Most Canadians agree with this; most jurors, if the case were put to them in this way, would be reluctant to find him guilty. Yet there is a very strong judicial aversion to jury nullification, an aversion that has led to a prohibition of encouraging nullification, and which in effect deprived Robert Latimer of his best defence.

Can this aversion, this denial of a basic civil liberty, be justified?

Sometimes judicial antipathy toward nullification is defended by citing the oath jury members take to uphold the law, which in Canada goes like this: "I swear to well and truly try and true deliverance make between our sovereign lady the Queen and the accused at the bar, whom I have in charge, and a true verdict give, according to the evidence, so help me God."

The first difficulty with this convoluted statement is that most jurors are unlikely to have any idea what it means. It is often explained by trial judges to mean something like "giving a true verdict according to the evidence." This is then taken, at least by some judges, as a commitment—a legal one—to render the verdict that follows from an exact reading of the law, not the verdict that might come from a sense of justice or a determination of real criminality.

But is it so? Is a true verdict necessarily one that follows the letter of the law? *True,* in normal language means not false, not counterfeit, and in accordance with fact and reality. A true verdict, then, is one that follows from all of the evidence and not from just some of it. For example, in the Latimer trials there was no doubt regarding the illegal act that he had committed, but the evidence also clearly showed he acted out of compassion, not malice. Motivation is absolutely crucial here—crucial to the determination of guilt and the assignment of criminality to the defendant. Motivation is part of the evidence.

If all the evidence points to guilt from a formal application of the law, but clearly leads to an unjust verdict, how can we consider that to be a "true verdict"? That is a false verdict according to the evidence. It is a verdict not in accordance with all of the evidence. Surely this broader sense of a "true verdict according to the evidence" is in the real spirit of why we have juries of peers; we want them to exercise their judgment as citizens on the case at hand.

Whatever the judiciary wishes to say about this, it seems clear that the oath does not take away the jury's right to nullify the law, or to seek justice.

Some judges still insist that nullification is somehow illegal. But how can it be deemed illegal if it is allowable under the law as an inherent right of jury members? There is no penalty for nullification, and no need for juries to explain their decisions. So in what sense can nullification be deemed illegal?

Some insist that, if it is not illegal, it is still somehow wrong. Such opposition sometimes appears to be based on a fear of diminishing respect for the law and of creating an anarchical system in which juries would generally be prone to disregard the law and "make up their own laws." But this is an unreasonable concern. In most trials there is little chance of nullification even being considered; the legal conflict is usually about whether or not the law was broken. A defence lawyer is unlikely, in the vast majority of cases, to want to take the position that his or her client may well be guilty, but should not be found so. That is indeed a risky proposition. Juries generally have a serious respect for the law, something that judges ought to urge them to have. It is only in rare cases that a nullification argument would have any traction with a jury; cases where a guilty verdict would, according to community standards, be unjust.

Diminishing respect for the law is more likely to be the result of the denial of justice, because of legal formalities, than it is to come from the exercise of jury independence. In blocking nullification as a defence, the judiciary is doing far more to erode respect for the law than any jury could do.

In the early 1970s, Dr. Henry Morgentaler was arrested and prosecuted in Quebec for performing illegal abortions. Even though he was technically in violation of the law, the jury refused to convict him. The Quebec Court of Appeals reversed the jury decision and Morgentaler went to jail for ten months, then was acquitted once again by a jury, on appeal. The federal government then passed an amendment to the Criminal Code which removed the right of judicial appeals to strike down jury decisions. Morgentaler then underwent a third jury trial and was acquitted again. He was arrested again in Ontario in 1983 and again acquitted by a jury, even though there was no question that he was technically guilty. Then, in 1988, the Supreme Court ruled that, according to the new Charter of Rights and Freedoms in Canada, the law banning abortions was unconstitutional.

Jury nullification can be appealed, on the grounds that it deviates from the law, but under Canadian law such an appeal cannot then be decided by the judiciary; it requires a jury trial once again. This can happen repeatedly until the judiciary decides that the juries have a point; that there is something wrong with the law, or at least with the application of the law. The four jury acquittals of Morgentaler illustrated clearly that the law in his case was out of step with what the Canadian public was prepared to tolerate from its legal system, and undoubtedly had a strong impact on the subsequent *Charter* interpretation that, in effect, legalized abortions in Canada. This is not to suggest that a verdict of not guilty in Latimer's case would have resulted in a similar legal change regarding euthanasia. Nevertheless it would point out the enormous value to the justice system of jury nullification (though a not-guilty verdict for Latimer might well have generated more discussion on the need for a compassionate homicide law in Canada).

Morgentaler's actions were viewed by his four juries as acts that should not be construed as crimes, even though they were technically illegal. They were viewed as acts of human kindness designed to help desperate women and to prevent them from taking dangerous back-alley measures to end their pregnancies.

Until the Morgentaler trials, nullification had been something that could be spoken of in the courtroom. In fact, at one point Morgentaler's lawyer said to the jury: "The judge will tell you what the law is. He will tell you about the ingredients of the offence, what the Crown has to prove, what the defences may or may not be, and you must take the law from him. But I submit to you that it is up to you and you alone to apply the law to this evidence and you have a right to say it shouldn't be applied."

Such a defence led to the acquittal of a man who was not a criminal, a man who performed a vitally important service to women and undoubtedly saved the lives of some, a man whose actions helped change an unjust law. This, for many people, was a high point in the administration of justice in Canada. Yet, the good consequences of the lawyer's plea—the freedom for Morgentaler and the legalization of abortion—were not sufficient to convince the Supreme Court that nullification as a defence ought to be permitted in the future.

On the contrary, and this is the great irony of the Morgentaler case, appealing for nullification subsequently became a forbidden defence. In the 1988 Morgentaler judgment declaring the prevention of abortions as being unconstitutional, Chief Justice G. B. Dickson felt obliged to crack down on nullification, citing the lawyer's appeal for nullification as being "so troubling that I feel compelled to comment."

What specifically were the concerns that the Chief Justice cited in prohibiting defence counsels from nullification and in blocking a basic civil liberty? One would think that such an intervention in the rights of individual defendants would have a powerful justification that would be compellingly articulated by the Supreme Court. At least, that was what I expected when I reviewed the Chief Justice's ruling. But his argument was a feeble one. And, in my view, it was presented in the arrogant and bullying style that too often substitutes for reason in judicial arguments.

Quoting a 1955 ruling in an English court, the Chief Justice supported the notion that the sole job of the jury is to interpret the "facts." But this idea has been a matter of debate in Britain for centuries. The judiciary in general would prefer a world in which the roles of judge and jury are simply delineated; that the judges interpret the law and the juries are "finders of fact." But juries, unquestionably, have a right that goes beyond finding the facts: a role that includes, at times, assessing the efficacy and appropriateness of the law for the case at hand. This has, in effect, been a principle of British law since the Magna Carta in 1215. That document established the right of all people accused of crimes to be tried by juries of their peers, thus blocking the arbitrary assignment of punishment by authorities (at the time it was to limit the powers of King John). But this revered principle would mean little if juries were constrained to follow any officially prescribed direction, if they were not free to make decisions they felt were right, regardless of the admonitions of any branch of government, lawmakers, or judiciary. Anything less would mean that assignment of guilt would revert back to those who make or administer laws. Absolute independence of juries is central to the idea that the state cannot be allowed to decide upon criminality. Although the judiciary is right to urge juries to follow the law, for the law derives normally from well-considered democratic processes and we should always respect it, the judiciary is wrong when it argues, as it frequently does, that juries are only "finders of facts." Juries must have the right to contravene the letter of the law when they believe that justice demands they do so.

Even the Chief Justice acknowledges this in his next and later statements, albeit grudgingly: "The jury is one of the great protectors of the citizen because it is composed of twelve persons who collectively express the common sense of the community. But the jury members are not expert in the law, and for that reason they must be guided by the judge on questions of law."

Yes, jurors are to be guided by the law, where they are inexpert, but how can they be "the great protectors of the citizen" if, in all circumstances, they accept exactly the conclusion the law leads them to? How does the "common sense of the community" then come into play? Interpreting the law is indeed a matter for experts. But we have a legal system in which the final arbitration of guilt or innocence is not simply a legal calculation; it is, as the Chief Justice acknowledges, the rendering of justice according to the common sense of members of the community. That is the purpose of the right of nullification. The idea is not that jurors in such cases are denying the judge's interpretation of the law, but that they are refusing to convict by that law. It is nullification of the law, not the interpretation or reinterpretation of the law.

The Chief Justice strongly opposes the actualization of the important jury right that he acknowledges. Why is nullification so dangerous, according to the Chief Justice? It is because:

> *A jury which is encouraged to ignore a law it does not like, could lead to gross inequities. One accused could be convicted by a jury who supported the existing law, while another person indicted for the same offence could be acquitted by a jury who, with reformist zeal, wished to express disapproval of the same law.*

There are a number of serious problems with this statement. For one thing the Chief Justice loads the language: he states his case in a prejudicial manner. He misrepresents the issue entirely by talking about a jury being "encouraged to ignore a law it does not like," as though the exercise of the legal right of juries to act as "one of the great protectors of the citizen" cannot in actuality be allowed because it may be wantonly employed. But any group of people in a position of responsibility may at some particular time behave improperly: the Supreme Court might even be found to be doing so. But we have juries and we have courts and appeal courts because we trust them to do what is right. In democratic states we trust ordinary citizens with the most important role in society, that of choosing our leaders. It does not always work out well but it is the best we can do. The election of an ineffective leader does not cause us to remove the voting rights of citizens. A misstep by a jury, or by the courts, or even by the Supreme Court, does not make us want to eliminate those bodies. They are all part of a complex balance of voices in the search for justice, and the possibility of one of them making an error does not, or should not, lead to undue limitations being placed on the designated role of any of them. That is precisely what the Chief Justice did in this ruling on juries and nullification, justifying his action with his mistrust of juries that might have "reformist zeal."

There are other problems here. Does the Chief Justice really mean to imply that legal consistency is more important than justice? Is it better that two people get convicted, unjustly, than one? Of course it is possible, as this statement seems to suggest, that a bunch of jurors could all be affected by some sort of excessive commitment to some idea that would bypass, rather than lead to, justice. But it seems unlikely that twelve people chosen at random would all be infected by the same sort of "zeal," and if they were it is likely that there would be some good reason for it, such as the unanimous opinion of four Morgentaler juries—forty-eight different citizens—that he was not a criminal.

The Chief Justice states: "Moreover, a jury could decide that although the law pointed to a conviction, the jury would simply refuse to apply the law to an accused for whom it had sympathy."

This is not an argument against nullification; it is the reason for allowing the possibility of nullification. If twelve citizens believe that it is wrong to convict someone, then they have the right and the obligation not to convict.

He continues: "Alternatively, a jury who feels antipathy towards an accused might convict despite a law which points to acquittal."

This again is a very weak argument. If such an unlikely situation did arise, there is an easy remedy. A judge has the right to dismiss cases which are not well supported in law.

The Chief Justice then addressed a common concern about nullification, a concern about the possibility of racist juries: "To give a harsh but I think telling example, a jury fueled by the passions of racism could be told that they need not apply the law against murder to a white man who had killed a black man. Such a possibility need only be stated to reveal the potentially frightening implications..."

But this concern, apparently based upon historical precedent in the American South, is misplaced. Jury nullification has been used much more extensively in fighting racism than it has in support of it. Nullification was frequently used by juries before the abolition of slavery in the United States to refuse to convict those who broke slavery laws, including slaves who escaped and were recaptured and those who helped them escape. It was a powerful tool used to fight legally sanctioned racism. The Chief Justice is evidently referring to cases in the early and mid-twentieth century, particularly that of Emmett Till in 1955, where it was alleged that juries refused to convict members of lynch mobs. But there were very few actual cases of this, and in those cases that did appear to involve the sanctioning of racism, there was much more going on than jury nullification (although, publicly, juries were given much of the blame). For one thing there is a question about the validity of the evidence provided in some cases: the juries may have lacked the necessary hard evidence for conviction, and instead of nullifying the law may well have been acting in accordance with the stipulation of "proof beyond reasonable doubt." Also, the juries in these cases were not representative of the community and consisted mostly of white males, because only registered voters could be selected as jurors and most blacks at the time did not meet that qualification. These were not the "juries of peers" that were called for in Magna Carta and have been a well-accepted component of justice ever since.

What the Chief Justice suggests as a "frightening" possibility, implying a historical precedent, is a misrepresentation of the past, and it raises further questions about his reasons for his prohibition of jury nullification. He has an antipathy for nullification, but not good reasons for denying it. Nullification has, historically, been a powerful force in combating the malign effects of bad laws.

It is true that juries can behave and have behaved badly. Most legally sanctioned practices have, at times, been used for bad purposes. The right to face one's accusers, for example, can result in the intimidation of witnesses. The right of *habeas corpus* can result in dangerous criminals being turned loose on the public. The possibility of abuse is not a reason to deny an important legal principle: that a jury may elect to act according to its conscience rather than the letter of the law. Nor is it sufficient reason to deny a defendant the important civil liberty of having the best possible defence.

Moreover, any group of people designated to carry out public business has the potential for bad behaviour; we cannot constrain such groups so that they are unable to function in an effective or fair manner. We must trust juries, prosecutors, and judges not to be racist; we cannot limit their options on the grounds that that they might be so. It is perhaps more likely that an individual judge might have particular prejudices—more likely than twelve jury members—but we do not prevent them from giving instructions to the juries because of that possibility (as perhaps happened in the Krieger case discussed earlier). Bad actions by judges in trials are subject to appeal, but so are bad actions by juries. If somehow, today, a jury of twelve racists was convened, and a racist decision resulted from this jury's nullification of the law, then an appeal would almost surely result in a retrial. Then, for the same bad decision to come forward again, another jury of twelve racists would have to be assembled. That would be a total of twenty-four racists, without a single voice of dissent, who would be needed to lead to the materialization of the "frightening possibility" expressed by the Chief Justice. Then another appeal leading to the same prejudiced verdict would require a jury of another twelve committed racists, and then, possibly, another twelve.

There is no guarantee that any players in the justice system will behave well; we can only hope that they will and have mechanisms for appeal if they do not. The one exception, of course, is the Supreme Court of Canada. To whom do we appeal if it is wrong? God?

The Chief Justice goes on to present an argument that, though badly stated, is not without merit: the law ought to be respected. But he goes much too far. Yes, general observance of the law is necessary in a civilized society, and observance is based upon knowledge of and respect for the importance of the rule of law. But respect for the law is not aided in cases where blind conformity to the law leads to a glaring injustice.

One of our most valued perspectives on crime and punishment was written by English jurist William Blackstone in his *Commentaries on the Laws of England* in the 1760s. Blackstone wrote: "Better that ten guilty persons escape than one innocent suffer." This has become known as Blackstone's formulation. The idea of a person being unjustly punished is an abhorrent one, and particularly abhorrent if it arises from avoidable rigidities in the law. Morgentaler was not a criminal, although the law said he was. His juries, because of their understanding of their right to nullify the law, largely protected him. Latimer was not a criminal either, but his juries, under the undue restrictions imposed on defence counsel by Chief Justice Dickson, were unable to protect him. Latimer's subsequent suffering has resulted in widespread anger and mistrust of Canadian law. Dickson's attempt to uphold the law in all circumstances has damaged, not protected, that which he rightly holds in such high regard.

The Chief Justice closes his argument here by stating that "recognizing this reality [the right of the juries to nullify the law] is a far cry from suggesting that counsel may encourage a jury to ignore a law they do not support or to tell a jury that it has the *right* to do so."

So it is not wrong for a jury to nullify the law, but it is wrong for a lawyer to counsel them to do so. Does this make any sense? A defence lawyer's responsibility is to present the strongest possible case for acquittal of his or her client. Central to that case may be asking a jury to act according to its conscience. But, according to the Chief Justice, in this ruling, a defence lawyer cannot even allude to such a possibility.

Ever since the Morgentaler ruling in 1988, with the Chief Justice's gratuitous and inconsistent statement on jury nullification, defence lawyers have taken his statement to be a prohibition of any appeal for such nullification. In effect this is a serious violation of the civil liberties of certain defendants; those who are technically guilty but who, like Morgentaler, are not criminals. All defendants ought to be entitled to the best possible defence. Since the Morgentaler ruling some defendants have been denied this—among them, Robert Latimer.

The Supreme Court of Canada, in this instance, has failed in its responsibility to protect the civil liberties of Canadian citizens.

The Latimer jury might well have been receptive to a defence based upon nullification. We can get a sense of this by looking for clues in the questions they brought back to the judge. After retiring to ponder their verdict, they came back with three questions, one of which is relevant here.

The jury members wanted to know if they could have a say in the sentencing, a pretty clear indication that they saw that Latimer was technically guilty, but did not want a severe sentence. This was a real turning point in the trial. With the jury excused again while an answer was being considered, a very significant debate occurred between Justice Noble, Prosecutor Neufeld, and Defence Counsel Brayford. The issue was whether or not the jury should be told something they apparently did not know—that a conviction of second-degree murder has a mandatory life sentence with a minimum of ten years before full parole. All three parties to the debate must have been fully aware of what was going on here. The judge undoubtedly suspected that if the jury knew of the severe penalty they might well choose to nullify the law by finding Latimer not guilty. Prosecutor Neufeld knew that his conviction was hanging in the balance. Brayford knew this was his client's only hope.

From the start, Justice Noble was clearly against revealing the truth about sentencing, a position strongly endorsed by the prosecutor. This was not because Noble was seeking to find Latimer guilty (his statement of support for Latimer in his making a case for a constitutional amendment on sentencing confirms that), but because he, like many judges, was against nullification, and would probably be embarrassed if such a thing happened in his court. At one point he said that the sentence was "none of their business."

When Justice Noble decided not only to refuse to tell the jury what they wanted to know, and then actually misled them, saying that they could talk to him about sentencing afterwards, he effectively ended any chance for nullification. There was much that happened after this, including appeals to the Saskatchewan Court of Appeal and then to the Supreme Court. But once the jury thought they could get a lenient sentence, and then turned in a verdict of guilty, the Latimer case was lost.

❧

Latimer's conviction and sentencing were appealed to the Supreme Court in 2001. Several issues formed the basis of the appeal, including the matter of a possible defence based on nullification. The appeal was based upon the reasonable notion that, if a defence lawyer cannot advocate nullification, neither can a judge try to block it. But the Court dismissed the relevance of this by claiming that "the trial judge's awkward but short response to the jury's inquiry did not prejudice the appellant," and that in any case the accused had no right to jury nullification!

It is regrettable that the Supeme Court chose to go even further than the

147

1988 Court did in denouncing nullification, making the odd argument that nullification is not a right at all:

> . . . *the accused has [no] right to jury nullification. How could there be any such 'right?' As a matter of logic and principle, the law cannot encourage jury nullification.*

The Court appears to be confused here. It is true that it would not make much sense for the courts to encourage nullification: a judge's proper role is to explain what the law says, not to suggest that it be circumvented. But the Court slides from the possibly legitimate argument that judges ought not to propose nullification, to the erroneous argument that defendants are not entitled to nullification if a jury believes it is warranted, to the highly dubious argument that the court cannot allow the defence to argue it before a jury.

In 1765 William Blackstone wrote: "Mankind will not be reasoned out of the feelings of humanity." Blackstone knew, 250 years ago, that the law must be more than a legal calculation. The judiciary in Canada today, however, not only discourages juries from consideration of any feelings of humanity, but defers to an arbitrary declaration of the Supreme Court of Canada—its prohibition of a defence based on the possibility of jury nullification—to further suppress the possibility of the expression of such feelings. Latimer's jury was not reasoned out of its feelings of humanity; it was prevented from expressing its feelings of humanity by a judicial ruling.

In 2009, American President Barack Obama, in discussing the qualities he would look for in a Supreme Court justice, said he sought a person who could think beyond "abstract legal theory or a footnote in a casebook" and have an understanding of "people's hopes and struggles, as an essential ingredient for arriving at just decisions and outcomes." The Canadian Supreme Court, in its delving into abstract legalities in regard to jury nullification, prevented a just decision and outcome for Robert Latimer.

Had the judicial restrictions on nullification not been so binding, Latimer's defence could have been far more compelling, and it is unlikely he would have been convicted at all. His legal nightmare should have ended there. It could have gone like this:

Ladies and Gentlemen of the jury,

We have before us, in this trial, a very unusual case, and one that puts you as jurors in a very difficult position. I sympathize with the agonizing choice you must make. For you, and you alone, will decide if Robert Latimer is to return to life with his family, his wife, and three surviving children, and his farm in northern Saskatchewan, after seven years of debilitating legal entanglement over the circumstances of his daughter Tracy's death, or if he is to go to prison on a conviction of second-degree murder, with its attendant minimum sentence of ten years before he is eligible for full parole.

It is you, and you alone, who have the right to make this decision, and it is a decision that, aside from all of the direction you will be given in regard to the law, you are entitled to make. You are entitled to make any decision you believe to be fair and just. The reasons for your decision and the deliberations that take place about your decision will, in our system of justice, remain within the confines of the chambers where your discussions take place. You have the absolute right to make whichever decision you choose to make, and in making your decision I ask only that you recognize that you are not simply servants of this court; more importantly, you are the servants of justice and mercy.

For that is the purpose of a jury of peers. If the law were simply a matter of calculating adherence to some law or another, then it would be best left to the experts who have been trained to make this calculation, and who are familiar with the letter of the law, and who have researched the vast legal literature to determine what precedents are most relevant to the case under consideration. Our justice system is rightly concerned with what has happened in similar cases, and with arguments that have been upheld in the past, and with consistency in the application of the law.

But the purpose of our legal system is not any of those things; it is the administration of justice. It is perhaps true that justice is most often served by adherence to strict legal procedures and precedents, but it is not always so. In some cases there are circumstances that are so unusual, and so compelling, that a strict and simplistic application of law is unjust. And I submit to you that that is the reason we have juries of citizens, like you, who are less expert in the law but who can see when the strict and simplistic application of a law is unjust. It is you who find yourselves in a situation, now, where such a consideration is one you must make.

There is no doubt that Robert Latimer intentionally ended the life of his daughter Tracy, and there is no doubt that the Criminal Code of Canada makes little allowance for mitigating circumstances. Were this case to be determined judicially, by those trained in the strict administration of the law, my client would be found guilty—guilty of second-degree murder, with the attendant minimum of ten years before full parole.

But, ladies and gentlemen of the jury, you are not the judiciary; you are twelve randomly selected citizens who are charged not simply with formal application of the law, for which there are better qualified people, but with deciding, according to your own perceptions and understandings, what is fair and just. You will be urged by my friend [the prosecuting attorney], whose job it is to administer the law as it stands, and by the Court, which has the same responsibility, to simply act according to a straightforward application of the law. But I urge you to see your role in a larger sense— that you have a responsibility to see that justice is the result here, not a formal interpretation of the law.

Robert Latimer did intentionally end the life of Tracy; of that there is no dispute. It is also the case that the Criminal Code allows little room for differences in such events. I want to put to you, however, that there are two very different situations that are covered by this law. One is an act of malice—a murder carried out selfishly and without regard for the consequences to the victim or the victim's friends and family. The other is an act of love, carried out for the benefit of the person who dies. The latter is much less common than the first, but as you can easily see it is difficult to call such an act murder. It is difficult to understand why these two extremely different acts can be regarded as the same thing, by the law.

One reason for the homicide law as it stands, though, is that we must have a way of ensuring that the ending of a human life is a most serious matter—as serious as anything that arises in our courts—and making little allowance for mitigating circumstances serves to emphasize this. It is good that anyone who contemplates ending the life of another realizes that he or she will be faced with the prospect of a very severe penalty. That is a good reason for the law as it stands.

But what do we do about those rare cases that are missed by our law, cases in which there are severe mitigating circumstances, where an application of a law designed to punish murderers is all we have to deal with, in a case that only in the most technical sense could be called a murder?

I am talking hypothetically for the moment. Whether or not you agree that Robert Latimer's act was an act of love rather than one of malice, and I will get back to that, you must, I think, agree that it is possible that such a thing could happen—that someone could end the life of another person for reasons of love or kindness, and that such a thing is the opposite of killing out of malice. Such things sometimes happen when a person becomes terminally ill and is in such agony that they are put out of their misery. There have in fact been cases of this where there is little doubt as to what happened, and murder could have been charged, but in most instances prosecution has been, for obvious reasons, avoided—avoided because of the recognition of the fact that mercy is not murder.

While it would be best if such acts of human kindness could be kept out of the courts, and resolved in some other way, we have before us what I will argue is a similar case, but one that has unfortunately come to trial, and is now being prosecuted under the Criminal Code for second-degree murder. This is a tool designed for dealing with acts of malice, and it does not serve the current situation well, if you accept that Robert Latimer's act was an act of love.

Was it an act of love? Obviously the argument I am making here only holds if you believe that it was. If you do not, then you will be obliged to find the defendant guilty, for his act would then be no different from other murders. But I put to you that it is clear that Robert Latimer and his wife Laura both loved their daughter, and both had been devoted to her for the twelve years she lived, and both were very upset by Tracy's deteriorating condition and horrifying and inescapable pain—and they no longer believed the arguments that her pain could be mitigated. There were no known pain killers other than Tylenol that she could take without worsening her convulsions, which racked her body several times every day, and caused the terrible agony of her hip joints dislocating. So there was no help to be found there—that is why the last doctor Tracy saw decided that her thigh bone had to be severed and the joint section removed, as a way to reduce the pain. The trouble was that the pain would not be relieved for some considerable time after the operation, and perhaps not at all. And then another such operation on her other leg would likely ensue, with more severe pain in a life marked by escalating pain. The Latimers were both appalled by the prospect of yet another radical operation on their daughter, particularly since they felt that Tracy had deteriorated in important ways after her three previous operations. The Latimers saw the new operations as not a cure for Tracy's pain, but as mutilation and further torture of their helpless daughter. Both of them came to the conclusion that Tracy's life had come to the point where it was no longer a life worth living—it had become an existence of ongoing torture.

It is important to understand at this point that Robert Latimer was not trying to escape his responsibilities in taking care of a severely handicapped daughter. He and Laura had been devoted parents for over twelve years. She was their daughter and they loved her. They could easily have let her die on many occasions—as when she choked on her food and had to have it removed from her throat. They could have sent her to an institution for care, but they felt she was better off in her own home with her own parents; and being somewhere else would not lessen her pain. Pushing the problem to somewhere out of sight was not an option for them—that would not have helped Tracy. Tracy's problem was their problem, and when the last devastating news was given to them by the orthopaedic surgeon they knew, in their hearts, that the only kindness they could now show to Tracy, the only true demonstration of love they could give her, was to take her out of her misery. Robert summoned up the courage to do this, courage that was bolstered by the fact that he was convinced it was the right thing to do, for Tracy.

There is no greater sadness a human can endure than the loss of a child, except—one can imagine—the witnessing of that child being tortured before it dies. Tracy had already lived longer than most children with her condition, and surely did not have much longer to go. Bob Latimer could have just let her go, as she surely would have before very long, and saved himself. But his conscience would not allow that—would not allow him to countenance the upcoming mutilation and further torture. Bob Latimer faced a terrible dilemma of the kind that, we all deeply hope, we will never be faced with. Few people have been. He could let her live and suffer, or he could end it all and give her peace at last. The first choice was terrible, because it meant ongoing torture for Tracy; the latter choice was terrible, not because of the consequences for Tracy—peace at last—but because of the agony of having to take such an action, with one's own child. Bob Latimer could get no help with this—there is no agency or support group for such things—there was no one, including his wife, whom he could even talk to about it, for fear of legal implications for anyone who knew. He did what he had to do, for Tracy.

There are those who would dispute this account of what happened but, I submit to you, they have various axes to grind. There are those who on religious grounds oppose the ending of a human life, whatever the circumstance. There are those who represent organizations for the disabled who oppose the ending of a human life because they feel that disabled people will be particularly vulnerable if such a thing is countenanced in any way. These voices, you should understand, would be equally vociferous whatever Tracy's condition was, whatever the horror of her ongoing life. So their arguments about the Latimer situation are compromised by their utter opposition to what happened, whatever the circumstance.

My friend, in prosecuting this case, has also suggested that things were not so bad, using a few comments made by Laura in a journal, the comments of a mother desperate to find something positive in Tracy's life—that she smiled or seemed to notice something, or that at one point she seemed to improve after her last operation—to suggest that Tracy's life was not so bad. But it is his job to present the evidence against my client as strongly as possible, and I certainly do not criticize him for doing so. But notice that even he does not argue that Robert Latimer's act was done for any reason but love.

It seems clear, ladies and gentlemen of the jury, from the testimony that has been brought forward, that Tracy's condition and Robert Latimer's reasons for ending her life were pretty much as I have described. This was an act of love, not an act of malice.

If you accept this argument, to this point, then let us go back to the problem with the law. Is it right to prosecute a man, for an act of mercy and love, in the same way that you would a man who killed out of malice? Would it be right to convict Robert Latimer and sentence him to the same punishment, which under the law cannot be less than ten years before parole, as real murderers, who kill others out of anger, hatred, or desire for personal gain?

I mentioned possible defences for second-degree murder, and, as you know, there are some. But for the most part they do not apply to this case. Robert Latimer was of sound mind when he committed the act, and it was not done in a momentary lapse or in a state of inebriation, or any such thing (all of these are possible defences against a charge of murder). The one defence that is open is that of necessity—that he had no other reasonable choice. This, in fact, would be a perfectly reasonable defence—except that legal precedents and strict interpretation of the law would probably narrow the use of such a defence to the point that it would be excluded by the Court. But Robert Latimer had no other reasonable choice. He could let Tracy live and suffer, or she could die and be at peace. He saw his decision as a moral necessity, regardless of the consequences to him.

But I'd rather describe Robert Latimer's situation in a different way. He did not act out of necessity—he could have let Tracy go on living for whatever time she had left. But, as Shakespeare writes, in Portia's great speech in The Merchant of

153

Venice, *"the quality of mercy is not strained."* *True acts of mercy are not those a person is forced to do, but those a person chooses to do. Tracy's death was not necessary, but it was merciful. We normally accord the highest respect to acts of mercy; there are few things that touch us so deeply. And acts of mercy that entail putting oneself at serious risk are of even greater merit.*

The Bible says, "blessed are the merciful, for they shall receive mercy." Sadly, in this world at least, such is not always the case. But you have an opportunity to see that, in this one case at least, that the merciful does receive mercy. It is up to you to make that decision, and I implore you to do so.

CHAPTER 11
JUSTICE AND MERCY

The problem of preventing a defence based upon jury nullification is not a problem with the law. As it stands now, there is no legislation that precludes it. It is, instead, a problem with how law enforcement is practiced and with how the Supreme Court of Canada has chosen to limit jury independence. Latimer's jury was sympathetic to him, but thought that it had no choice but to convict. Justice Noble essentially told them that. One juror afterwards said he did not like the outcome, but the jury had no choice. Simply allowing a defence lawyer to present that possibility—pointing out the jury's legal right not to convict, whatever the evidence—would probably have avoided this lengthy legal debacle.

It seems likely that Latimer did not fully understand this, or the bind that his defence lawyer was in. He said after his conviction that he had thought at least one of the jurors would have been on his side, "but I guess not." But this was clearly a misunderstanding of what had happened: he apparently believed that if the jurors were on his side they would have supported him. But he might well have had all twelve supporting him. It was not that they were against him, it was that they thought they were legally obliged to find him guilty. After his second conviction he told reporters that, "I don't believe the jury had a good enough idea of just what Tracy's problems were." Again, this is misreading the situation. The jury appeared to be in full sympathy with Latimer's position. They just thought they had no choice.

It is not likely that his misreading of this situation hurt Latimer: his lawyer was acutely aware of the problem and fought hard to overcome it, but there was little he could do. Latimer's lack of legal sophistication did hurt him at other times. Although a lack of sophistication ought not to harm a person who is caught in legal proceedings—that, after all, is why we have lawyers—there is a limit in a free country to how much a person can be protected. No one has or should have the right to stop Latimer from engaging in a hopeless legal quest; no one can force him to apply for clemency. No one can force him to accept that the jurors who convicted him were not necessarily hostile to him. Nevertheless, law enforcement officials ought to take great care not to take undue advantage of a straightforward and ordinary man, however tempting it might be for them to do so. Allowing Latimer to talk without a lawyer, even though he was given many chances to call one, is an example of an instance when the police could have insisted upon a lawyer being present.

There are a number of other disturbing questions about how Latimer was treated by the Canadian justice system. For example, in all cases there is supposed to be a presumption of innocence. One would hope that law enforcement officials would have at least acknowledged the possibility that he had acted of mercy and tempered their prosecutorial zeal to some degree.

Although the initial arresting officers in the Latimer case showed some kindness to him, the police and the prosecutor were subsequently unfair, and illustrated both their assumption of guilt and their mistrust of the jury system by tampering with the jury pool in Latimer's first trial. The prosecutor in that trial, Randy Kirkham, seemed overeager in charging Latimer with murder: simply charging him with manslaughter rather than murder would have eliminated the unreasonable sentencing requirement, and most of the subsequent legal wrangling would probably never have happened. A manslaughter charge would have been much more appropriate in the circumstance; murder is usually regarded as taking a life with malice, and there was never the slightest hint of malice in Latimer's action. And the penalty for manslaughter, unlike that for murder, is not constrained by an arbitrary minimum imprisonment. The one-year sentence recommended by his judge and jury would not likely have been appealed, Latimer would have been released from prison in 2001 or 2002, and he would not be faced with the lifetime parole condition that attends conviction for murder.

There are many elements in our justice system that are unfair, including the cost of providing oneself with a defence when prosecuted by the Crown. There are various forms of legal aid, but if someone is faced with the prospect of going to jail for life, that person will want to have the best available defence lawyers, who may not be the ones available through legal aid. Latimer supporters had no campaign to raise funds for his defence, but they did not need to. In one of my conversations with Latimer he said that unsolicited donations of about $400,000 were sent in by people who thought he was being treated unfairly. But one wonders how many lower-profile cases are defended inadequately, without the benefit of such support. We have in Canada a medical care system that ensures that no one is ruined by disastrous medical costs, but the same is not true in the legal system. A person can be prosecuted by the Crown, found not guilty, and still be responsible for ruinous legal expenses.

Looking at the costs of the Latimer prosecution in a different way, a lot of taxpayer money was wasted. Latimer's lengthy legal proceedings cost millions, perhaps tens of millions, to no real purpose. It is hard to see that the relentless prosecution and massive expenditure have, to date, made the country better in any way, or done anyone any good. It behooves us to find a better way of handling such matters.

It may, of course, be necessary to spend large sums of public money on legal matters that are not clearly, or are inadequately, covered by existing laws, or where such laws are not consistent with public opinion. The Morgentaler trials served the extremely valuable purpose of stopping prosecutions for abortion; that was public money well spent. But if we do not learn from high-profile and expensive legal proceedings, as we did from Morgentaler, then the money is wasted. And so far, as a society, we seemed to have learned nothing from the Latimer case. There has been no effort by the Supreme Court of Canada to protect our civil liberties and amend the Court's arbitrary and unfair stance on jury nullification. Nor has there been a serious effort by our politicians to amend our arbitrary and unfair laws on assisted suicide and euthanasia, or to seek new legislation on compassionate homicide.

Our laws on assisted suicide and euthanasia are by their nature discriminatory, because they grant rights and administer punishment in an inconsistent and unfair manner. We hope to have laws that are designed in a thoughtful and rational way, based on principles of fairness and equal treatment for all. But discriminatory laws come as a result of fear, prejudice, and political influence. They inevitably are inconsistent and fall short of the standard of reasonableness and fairness we might otherwise hope for. The famous Sue Rodriguez case showed how the assisted suicide law in Canada discriminates against severely disabled persons by denying them the legal right to suicide held by others, simply because a severely disabled person requires assistance, which is legally denied. It is unfortunate that the Supreme Court refused Rodriguez's appeal (by a five to four vote) and Canada lost another opportunity to redress unfair and evidently unconstitutional legislation on assisted suicide. The law is unconstitutional because it discriminates against the severely disabled.

❦

We need a better way to deal with the very real and increasingly common end-of-life dilemmas we face in our society. Assisting suicide is given a severe penalty in Canadian law, and, as we have seen, euthanasia is treated as murder.

The prohibition of assisted suicide results in the imposition of an intolerable cruelty upon those who desperately want to die because they have reached a point where they feel life is truly no longer worth living. Legalizing assisted suicide would be straightforward: over time, people would have to express a strong and consistent wish to end their lives, and they would have to undergo an independent assessment to ensure that they were not being pushed into this action, and that the decision was not the result of some temporary depression. Terminal illness might also be a requirement. Laws like this have already been passed in Oregon and Washington.

The related issue of euthanasia, which implies the ending of a life without consent, at least at the time of dying, is a much more problematic issue. A common and fairly widely accepted form of euthanasia is called passive euthanasia, and simply involves the cessation of life-preserving medical interventions. Ideally this is done when it is the expressed wish of the patient not to be kept alive under certain circumstances, through a living will, or a "do not resuscitate" order, or some such document. This is voluntary passive euthanasia. In the absence of such a document the decision becomes more difficult, but can still be made, based on family members' and friends' recollections of the patient's expressed wishes. In cases where a patient has expressed the desire to be kept alive at all costs, because of personal beliefs, then that, of course, is also honoured.

A more difficult end-of-life issue is that of "active" euthanasia, where steps are taken actively and intentionally to end a human life, as in the Latimer case. This is strictly illegal, whatever the circumstances, whether voluntary (prior consent given) or not, and is so in most of the world. The difference between turning off a valve to end life support and turning one on to end a life changes a commonly accepted medical action to murder. Yet it is not terribly difficult to imagine an enlightened law that would allow voluntary active euthanasia; it would be relatively easy to set up conditions requiring uncoerced prior consent. For example, a person might state, in writing, before incapacitation, that he or she does not wish to continue to exist in a vegetative state. Those wishes, and this form of voluntary euthanasia, ought to be respected, whether or not dying involves shutting off life support (passive) or taking some more direct action (active).

The most difficult situations of all are those involving someone like Tracy Latimer, who not only could not express her wishes, but would have been unable to understand the matter in the first place. Should it be that the merciful ending of the life of such a child, in worsening and hopeless agony, depends upon the courage of a parent to commit an illegal act, an act that imposes the most severe of penalties? Can we imagine laws that would safely allow such instances of active non-voluntary euthanasia? Simply doing it, as Latimer did, is not acceptable: it is necessary for society to "denounce" the action, as the Supreme Court said, regardless of circumstances. Although he was angry with the Court for "deciding to send me to prison for a long time," the Supreme Court and, in fact, all of the courts involved, had little choice but to enforce the law as it is written. A person simply cannot be allowed to make such decisions with impunity.

There are two ways, besides the possibility of jury nullification, that situations like that faced by the Latimers' could be addressed in a more balanced manner. One is the creation of a law covering compassionate homicide, a law that recognizes the possibility of compassionate mitigating circumstances. The other is to pass legislation that would permit, in extreme circumstances, non-voluntary, active euthanasia. This would necessarily be very carefully worded and cautious legislation with strict guidelines; it is possible that even Tracy's case would not qualify. But it would give desperate people like Robert and Laura Latimer at least the opportunity to pursue a legal remedy for their daughter's terrible plight.

❧

A few years ago, there were some reasons for optimism regarding new and more permissive end-of-life legislation in Canada. The 2004 trial of Evelyn Martens for assisted suicide had resulted in a verdict of not guilty, even though she had attended the two suicides in question. The Academy Award for best film that same year went to Clint Eastwood's *Million Dollar Baby*, a very sympathetic look at assisted suicide. The Academy Award for best foreign film, again in 2004, was given to a Spanish film, *The Sea Inside*, also a most supportive treatment of the same topic. The Canadian film *The Barbarian Invasions*, another sympathetic treatment of assisted suicide, won in the same category a year earlier. While these beautifully made films undoubtedly brought the attention of many people to some of the problems associated with the prohibition of assisted suicide and euthanasia, the socially conservative wave that subsequently engulfed both Canada and the United States probably killed any hope of legislative change, although the passage of new permissive legislation in Washington State in 2008 was a very encouraging development.

There are five jurisdictions in the world that have laws specifically permitting assisted suicide and/or euthanasia, and a sixth, the American state of Montana, has a recent judicial decision ruling assisted suicide legal, though that is, at the time of this writing, under appeal.

Both assisted suicide and euthanasia have been practised in the Netherlands since 1985, with a law passed in 2002 to codify the practices. Belgium passed a similar law in 2002. In both countries physicians, under certain conditions, may administer a lethal injection of drugs (euthanasia) or assist suicide by providing drugs that can be self-administered (assisted suicide). The request must be freely made and unchanging, and the suffering must be hopeless and unbearable (though not necessarily terminal). A second physician, who has talked to the patient directly and independently, must concur in the decision.

Switzerland has permitted both physician and non-physician assisted suicide since 1941, based upon an interpretation of their suicide law. In 2001, a law was passed that makes both assisted suicide and euthanasia illegal, but it does not penalize the former and penalizes the latter only if it is carried out "from selfish motives." Candidates must be mentally competent and suffering from an incurable disease. Switzerland is the only jurisdiction where non-residents may get assistance in suicide, through an organization called Dignitas. Lethal doses of drugs are provided by a physician or by a right-to-die society, such as Dignitas, which usually insists on medical verification of a terminal illness. Many people travel from other places, particularly from other European countries, for this service. There are long waiting lists and some estimate that two out of three people committing suicide in Switzerland are foreigners.

Oregon passed its *Death with Dignity Act* (*DWDA*) in 1994 and it was enacted on October 27, 1997, after delay by a legal injunction. While the act was initially passed by a very narrow margin, it was reconfirmed by a vote of sixty percent. The act permits assistance in dying, which it does not refer to as suicide, probably for some political reason, through the voluntary self-administration of lethal medications prescribed by a physician. The patient must be eighteen years of age or older, a resident of Oregon, capable, and diagnosed with a terminal illness that will lead to death within six months. There are a number of steps involved in the process, including confirmation from a second physician.

Detailed records are kept of the patients in Oregon. In the first year, 1998, there were twenty-four prescriptions given and sixteen subsequent suicides. By 2007 there were eighty-five prescriptions given and forty-five suicides from those prescriptions, plus three more from prescriptions given in a previous year. All patients cite loss of autonomy as the reason they wish to die, and most also mention the loss of activities that made life enjoyable, and the loss of dignity. Of every 10,000 deaths in Oregon, a statistical 15.6 occur under the *DWDA*.

In 2001, US Attorney General John Ashcroft launched a constitutional appeal against the Oregon law, taking it all the way to the American

Supreme Court, but the law was upheld. Then, in the elections held on November 4, 2008, Washington State passed *Initiative 1000*, similar to Oregon's *DWDA*, by a margin of 59 per cent.

There are other countries that do not address assisted suicide and euthanasia specifically in their laws, but permit some such actions in practice. Sweden and Norway generally give lighter sentences to "offenders"; Sweden charges them with manslaughter rather than murder. Finland is generally quite tolerant. Germany bans euthanasia but appears to be tolerant of assisted suicide, which it does not address in its criminal code. France regards assisted suicide as illegal but also does not do much about it. Italy legally forbids it. Danish law does not address it. In 2008 the Luxembourg parliament voted to legalize euthanasia, as practised in the Netherlands and Belgium, but the measure has been blocked by Grand Duke Henri, whose signature is required on all laws. This may precipitate a change to the constitution in that country.

Since 1936, some English politicians have been struggling to change a repressive law that requires, as does Canadian law, a penalty of up to fourteen years in prison for assisting suicide. English law, also like Canadian law, has decriminalized suicide while maintaining the illegality of assisted suicide. Canada, then, is not the only country with the odd practice of calling assistance in a non-crime a crime.

In early 2010 the Director of Public Prosecutions in England issued guidelines to clarify when someone assisting in a suicide might not be prosecuted. These were:

1. *The victim reached a clear, voluntary decision to commit suicide.*
2. *The suspect was wholly motivated by compassion.*
3. *The suspect reported the suicide to the police and fully assisted enquiries.*

Specifically excluded was any consideration of the condition of the victim. While these new guidelines might be a step in the right direction it is hard to see how they will help much. Would anyone dare report assisting a suicide, and fully cooperate in the investigation, with such lack of clarity in regard to prosecution—having to prove that he or she was "wholly motivated by compassion?"

Would it not be better simply to establish beforehand whether the conditions were met, through a panel of disinterested observers, under a law that allowed controlled assisted suicide? Why are legislators so afraid to take this simple step? The good thing about the new guidelines in England is that they do establish that assisted suicide is not necessarily a crime. In many other jurisdictions, including Scotland, Hungary, and Russia, assisted suicide and euthanasia remain strictly illegal; as, of course, they are in Canada.

Canada would appear to be one of the less progressive countries in regard to end-of-life issues. Hope was raised when a senate committee was appointed in the nineties to consider related matters, but its report, "Of Life and Death," looked mostly at issues around palliative care and the need for national consistency. It said little about the substantive and crucial legal issues. It did make one recommendation relevant to the discussion here: that the Criminal Code be amended to provide for a less severe punishment for "compassionate homicide"—less severe than the punishment for murder. This desirable proposition, probably resulting from the evident injustice of the Latimer prosecution, which was occurring at the time the committee was meeting, has been ignored by the Canadian Parliament.

There have been a number of attempts by certain politicians in Canada to pass modest laws regarding end-of-life issues. The first, *Bill C-203*, was bought forward by Robert Wenman, Member of Parliament for Fraser Valley West, on May 16, 1991, and would have protected physicians from criminal liability when, at the request of a patient, they do not activate or continue treatment, thereby hastening death, or where they do not make attempts to prolong life, except at a patient's request that they do so. It also would have protected physicians in cases where terminal sedation hastened death. This bill was sent to a legislative committee that listened to twenty-five witnesses, then permanently ended proceedings, apparently because of negative testimony (it was called the "euthanasia bill" by some) as well as the religious beliefs of some of the committee members. A similar bill was introduced on March 22, 1993 by Port Moody–Coquitlam–Port Coquitlam MP Ian Waddell, but this too soon died.

In 2005, Francine Lalonde, Bloc Québécois MP for La Pointe-de-l'Île, introduced *Bill C-407*, "An Act to amend the Criminal Code (the right to die with dignity)." This bill, more ambitious than the previous ones, would have legalized assisted suicide and euthanasia under certain controlled conditions. The bill was debated in the House of Commons on October 31, 2005, but subsequently died.

Why, we might well ask, is Canada not more progressive in this? It is not for lack of public support. Polls consistently show support for more permissive and less punitive legislation. In February of 2010 an Angus Reid poll showed that sixty-seven per cent of all Canadians support legalizing euthanasia, while only twenty-three per cent oppose it.

Alexis de Tocqueville was concerned, in *Democracy in America*, about "the tyranny of the majority." But that is not the problem we are facing here. Instead, we are being tyrannized by a small, very strident, very aggressive minority—a minority that systematically and at times viciously attacks any individual or group or politician proposing enlightened legislation in regard to these issues. It is not an odd minority of us who want change; it is most of us. It is an unreasoning minority, with particular axes to grind, that has hijacked the agenda.

We need to take back the initiative on end-of-life issues, as the citizens of Oregon did in bringing about their *Death with Dignity Act*, and as the citizens of Washington State did in 2008. If we took just such a modest step to fulfill the wishes of most Canadians, we should also consider, as the senate committee report "Of Life and Death" recommended, a Criminal Code amendment in regard to compassionate homicide. Such an amendment would not absolve those who cause the death of another of responsibility for that act, but it would permit the defence of compassionate mitigating circumstances.

Instead of being in a backwater, Canada could lead the world by creating progressive end-of-life legislation. We could get started by adopting the limited ideas that have won public support in Oregon and Washington. Or we could go much further and create ground-breaking legislation based upon a humane, rational, and compassionate assessment of real human needs.

AFTERWORD

Many problems seem impossible to solve. There are natural disasters that are beyond our control; many social, political, and economic problems that seem hopeless and out of our reach. We are mostly helpless in the face of many unpredictable national and global forces. We all want to build a better world but we do not, for the most part, know how to go about doing so.

But there are some things we can change for the better. Canada is a democracy and we, as citizens, have the power to make changes—to build a more just and merciful society—if we know what we want to do.

And Canadians do know what they want to do, at least in regard to euthanasia. The behaviour of the jury in the Latimer case, and of the juries in Henry Morgentaler's four trials, is strong evidence of that. And the fundamental good will and kindness of the Canadian people are evident in many different ways, including the widespread sympathy that was shown to Latimer, in letters, in newspaper articles, and in financial support. Every Christmas for many years after the death of his daughter Tracy, Robert Latimer received an anonymous Christmas card enclosing a $1,000 bill. He received many generous donations to help pay for his legal costs, because many Canadians recognized that, though the justice system was treating him like a criminal, he was not a criminal. Canadians recognize that Latimer acted out of love and human compassion, not malice. And polls consistently show not only strong support for Latimer but also for legalizing euthanasia.

It is time now for us, as a people, to take some stronger action. The laws and the ways in which they are enforced will always be imperfect. But when we see imperfections that are fundamentally unmerciful and which lead to serious injustices, we need to ensure that changes are made. The persecution and prosecution of Henry Morgentaler led the Canadian people, and their politicians, to realize that prosecuting doctors for performing abortions is wrong. Let us hope that the persecution and prosecution of Robert Latimer will now generate a similar demand for change. Let us hope that something positive will come out of his otherwise pointless years of suffering, and that his courageous act of mercy will help lead us toward a more just and humane society.

ACKNOWLEDGEMENTS

Thanks go first to Gwyneth Evans, the person who has helped me so much throughout the years of working on this manuscript; she is really a co-author. Many thanks as well to those who have taken time to read the manuscript at various stages and give me their advice: John Robert Colombo, Brian Finnemore, Jean Irwin, Shirley Johnson, and Bob Rowan. Special thanks to John Dixon and Jason Gratl not only for their comments and help but for taking the action that resulted in Latimer getting released from prison. And thanks to Mark Brayford and Marj Mosienko for help in building a more complete picture of the events that transpired.

Diane Young, Lorimer's editorial director, did outstanding work in helping to organize and improve the final manuscript. I was fortunate indeed to have such a skilled person to work with.

I also wish to express my deep appreciation to Robert Latimer for his help with much of this book, and to join with the millions of Canadians who, in recognizing his honesty, bravery, and compassion, wish him and his family all the best for the future.

NOTES

INTRODUCTION

Why would a determined secularist quote from the Bible in the first line in his book?

The words of the Bible are not the property of any religious group or of any individual or group, but part of our cultural heritage and as such belong to all of us. These particular words illuminate some deeply held human feelings about mercy—that mercy represents the best in human behaviour and that a merciful attitude is sorely needed in a world dominated by passion for violence and revenge, rather than compassion for human beings struggling with their imperfections. We will obtain mercy when we are generous in giving it, not because some higher being will bestow it upon us, but because it is a matter of personal redemption. All caring people regret instances of their own gratuitous and often unthinking cruelty, and of misdeeds of many different kinds, instances where we have made the world and the experience of our fellow humans worse, not better. Acts of mercy help us forgive ourselves for these transgressions: we obtain mercy from giving it.

CHAPTER 1

The description of Wilkie was taken from the Wilkie website (townofwilkie. com) and from discussions with Robert Latimer.

The statement that "Robert Latimer is one of those good people" derives in part from my own observations of him and the casual comments of others who knew him. The perception of Latimer as a good man is also derived from statements given by his trial judge, Justice G.E. Noble (Chapter 2) and by Saskatchewan Chief Justice E. D. Bayda (Chapter 3), and from my own discussions with some friends and relatives. Supportive comments from his neighbours, showing the high regard in which the Latimers were held, were reported in the *Calgary Sun* on November 21, 1994:

Responding to the negative comments of people from outside their community, Latimer's farming neighbour, sixty-nine-year-old Wilson Barker said: "I don't know how people can talk so badly about him when they have no idea what he was going through."

Another neighbour, Elvin Risling, 70, said, "Bob's a very honest man. . . He's a kindly man, both to his family and neighbours, always lending a helping hand."

Reverend Ken Shrag of the Wilkie United Church, which the Latimers attended, urged church members to write letters to their government representative, asking that Latimer be considered for clemency. Shrag said: "I believe Bob and Laura should be treated with compassion and understanding."

Even schoolteacher Brennan Merkosky, a Catholic who is against the taking of any life, said: "I think you've got to search your soul to get around that for [Latimer]. You don't want to see it so black and white."

The phrase that came up frequently in regard to Latimer was "salt of the earth," a phrase originating in the Bible in Matthew 5:13, generally meaning a person who is thought to be kind, reliable, decent, honest, and unpretentious. Chief Justice Bayda used the phrase salt of the earth (see Chapter 3), as did Dr. R. P. Menzies, the forensic psychiatrist who spent many hours talking to Latimer and testified "He struck me as a candid individual, a responsible individual, thought seriously before he acted, he wasn't impulsive. He wasn't prone to angry behaviour, sort of salt of the earth type of person" (Page 640, Transcript of Court Proceedings [hereafter referred to as Court Proceedings] for the second trial, now available at robertlatimer.net).

Corporal Hartle, the RCMP officer who first attended the Latimer residence after Tracy died, and who first suspected that this might have been a mercy killing, seemed to have little doubt that Latimer was a good person, stating in his subsequent request for a search warrant that "I believe Robert Latimer's motive was humanitarian in nature, due to the deceased's pain, deterioration, and the possibility of institutionalization was unacceptable to them" (page 675, Court Proceedings).

Comments about the Latimer family and farm come from my discussions with Robert Latimer and from telephone interviews with Robert's half-sister Marj Mosienko, who lives in Ottawa.

Commentary about Latimer's 1974 conviction on sexual assault is presented very critically on a number of websites such as LifeSiteNews.com (Nov. 28, 1997). These commentaries suggest that Latimer is not such a decent fellow after all, with a pattern of bad behaviour. The trouble with this argument is that not only was the assault charge against the very young Latimer successfully appealed, the judge in that trial happened to be the same Justice E.D. Bayda, who later, as the Saskatchewan Chief Justice, wrote the stirring account of Latimer that is presented here in Chapter 3 saying that, among other very positive things, Latimer was "a loving, caring, nurturing person." Bayda, we can safely assume, knows much more about both the 1974 trial and Latimer's 1994 trial (about the death of Tracy), and about Latimer, than the critics do.

Information about the birth and subsequent life of Tracy Latimer comes mostly from the Court Proceedings, and particularly from the defence examination of Laura Latimer (pages 9–516) and the testimony of Dr. Anne Dzus (pages 306–339). Quotes from Robert Latimer can be found in his many letters to the Supreme Court of Canada in 2001 and 2003, which can be found in his compilation of letters and documents called "My Attempts to Understand the Supreme Court's January 18/2001 Decision." The version I have used is dated September 2005. Some of this document is online at robertlatimer.net. Information about Tracy's stay at the North Battleford Group home came from trial testimony from employees of the home (pages 385–450).

CHAPTER 2

The quote from Justice G. E. Noble, about Latimer's love for and devotion to Tracy, comes from his sentencing statement on December 1, 1997, following the second trial, where he took the bold step of agreeing with the jury's request to grant a constitutional exemption to the normal ten-year minimum sentence and give only a one-year sentence. Noble gives a powerful argument for this, but his decision was subsequently overturned by the Saskatchewan Court of Appeal on November 23, 1998. Noble's full statement is available at robertlatimer.net, under court transcripts, or 1994 No. 37 J.C.B.

The quote from Saskatchewan Chief Justice E. D. Bayda about Latimer being "a nurturing, caring, giving . . . responsible parent" comes from his opinion in the appeal to the conviction and imposition of a ten-year minimum sentence in Latimer's first trial. Bayda agreed with the other two members of the Appeals panel in regard to upholding the guilty verdict, but differed with them on the matter of the constitutional exemption. Like Noble, who was to come to the same conclusion in his sentencing verdict after the second trial, Bayda supported the exemption. His statement was so compelling and powerful that his comments about Latimer are reproduced here in Chapter 3. The full decision from the Appeals Court can be found at 1998 CanLII 12388 (SK C.A.).

The statement by Latimer regarding how he and Laura could not tolerate cruelty to Tracy is among many such statements he made in letters to the Supreme Court in 2001 and 2002 in his compilation of letters and documents noted above.

The commentary about Latimer saying nothing and pretending to fall asleep after Laura mentioned Dr. Kevorkian comes from the trial testimony of Dr. Menzies (pages 637 and 638 of the Court Proceedings).

Information regarding the events of October 24, 1993, the day Tracy died, and the subsequent police investigation leading to Latimer's arrest on November 4, 1993, comes mainly from the trial testimony of Corporal Hartle, Sergeant Lyons and Sergeant Conlon of the RCMP and others related to the RCMP investigation (pages 61 to 292 of the Court Proceedings).

When Laura, Robert's sister Pat and the three Latimer children had to vacate the house while a search was being carried out on November 4, I have assumed that they all went to the RCMP detachment in Battleford, although this is not clear. Laura did see Robert there at 3:30 p.m., but she and the others may have spent some or all of the several hours they were away from the house at some other location.

The curious difference between Hartle and Latimer about what happened or did not happen when Robert and Laura supposedly met in private in their bedroom to talk about cremation came to light in a discussion I had with Latimer.

Latimer's discomfort with lawyers was reflected many times in things he said and did, most notably in his refusal to consult a lawyer during his initial interrogation and through to his getting no legal advice for his parole hearing or even, at first, being willing to prepare an appeal of the parole decision. I asked him if he had received any advice on how to present himself to the Board, or if he had considered such a thing or would do so for any future hearing, or if he would consider having a lawyer with him in the future (as is allowed at hearings). But clearly he was not interested. In Mark Brayford's closing remarks to the jury he slightly ruefully alludes to Latimer's comment in a television interview that "I don't necessarily agree with Mark Brayford's way of handling this," although he does add "but in the end I do, because I am really lost in these areas" (page 680, Court Proceedings). This reveals Latimer's ambivalence about his plight. He thought he should really be taking care of things himself, but at the same time realized at some level that he was not competent to do so. Although I never directly asked him this, I suspect that he feels that he was not well served by his legal counsel, and that if he had addressed the jury directly, and just told them the truth, he would have fared better. I do not think he ever had any deep understanding of the legal problems faced by Brayford. As evidenced by his many letters to the Supreme Court and to various politicians, Latimer did not really grasp the gist of the Supreme Court's rejection of his appeal. He speaks of their decision "to send me to jail for a long time," as though it had been a personal rather than a legal decision by the Court. He seems to think that he can get them to reverse their decision by claiming that false evidence about "more effective pain medication" had been presented to them. This quest, taking of matters into his own hands, is discussed in Chapter 4. It was not, however, as though he did not have competent counsel representing him at the Supreme Court hearing, counsel who somehow missed the point of defence that Latimer thinks is so crucial. As well as Mark Brayford, he had Canada's best known trial lawyer, Edward Greenspan.

CHAPTER 3

The ruling by Justice Wimmer was that police statements obtained from Latimer were permissible (1994 CanLII 5057 SK Q.B.). Wimmer based this decision on his perception that "Latimer was well briefed as to his right to legal counsel."

Sources for the first trial are sketchy, but some information can be found in the proceedings of a hearing to consider the requests of two organizations to attend the appeal of the first trial (CanLII 3921 SK C.A.), and in the proceedings of the appeal itself (1995 CanLII 3993 SK C.A.).

The latter source also contains the rebuke of Prosecutor Randy Kirkham for the intemperate language he used in describing Latimer. In part Kirkham's claim that Latimer was "foul, cold, calculating . . ." was repudiated by the Appeal panel in saying "we are not to be taken as in any way approving some of the comments of Crown counsel" and then perhaps more strongly in Justice Bayda's words quoted later in this chapter, in direct contradiction to Kirkham, including such phrases as "the actor was a nurturing, caring, giving, respectful, law-abiding responsible parent of the victim."

Other remarks from Kirkham's closing address to the jury were taken from chninternational.com/tracybod.htm.

References to the interview with Amy Jo Ehman come from several different sources, including the website for the Council of Canadians with Disabilities: ccdonline.ca/en/humanrights/endoflife/latimer/reflections/chronology. Her videotaped interview with Latimer was played in court but is not included with the Transcript of Proceedings. A reference to Wilson Barker and his posting of bail is also here.

Regarding the Supreme Court's 2008 judgment on Charter remedies, it ruled that judges cannot grant case-by-case "constitutional exemptions" from mandatory minimum sentences which too harshly punish one or more individuals. *R. v. Ferguson*, (2008) S.C.J. No. 6.

In regard to the jury-tampering issue that led to the ordering of a new trial by the Supreme Court, Latimer's claim that five of the jurors had been screened may be inaccurate. Others have claimed it was two or three. But regardless of the numbers it appeared to the Supreme Court that this was an improper action by Kirkham and the RCMP. A copy of the questionnaire was retrieved by the Latimers and it has been reproduced on the Latimer website: robertlatimer.net. Included were questions such as,

Religion _____ *Strong* ____ *Weak* ____

Pro-life _____ *Pro-choice* _____

Any family disabilities: (Describe) _____

Any disabled close associates: (Describe) _____

Mercy Killing Opinion, if any: _____

On June 27, 1996, the *Globe and Mail* announced that Randy Kirkham was being charged with attempting to obstruct justice. Kirkham was suspended with pay for about a month and then without pay. On June 19, 1998, a Saskatchewan court found Kirkham not guilty, because it could not prove intent to obstruct justice. There are various commentaries on this strange series of events. One sympathetic to Kirkham is: theinterim.ca/august98/16latimer.html

A site that briefly describes Kirkham's defence and which supports Latimer's claim that five of the resulting jurors had been screened by police, is: lifesitenews.com/ldn/1998/may/98051303.html

The Supreme Court judgment to order a retrial is at 1997 CanLII 405 (S.C.C.).

My quoting of Latimer in this chapter, and elsewhere in the book, comes from my many discussions with him between 2005 and 2010, sometimes from casual discussion, sometimes from interviews. Comments about the perception that some had of Hartle at the first trial were provided by Marj Mosienko, Robert's half-sister.

The long quote from Justice Bayda is in the judgment of the Saskatchewan Court of Appeal 1995 CanLII 3993 (SK C.A.)

The official charge against Latimer in his second trial is taken from the Court Proceedings, Page 2. Errors in the original document—the date of Tracy's death and the Criminal Code reference—were corrected.

The jury selection process is covered on pages 3–13 of the Court Proceedings.

Justice Noble's charge to the jury is on pages 21–30 of the Court Proceedings.

Prosecutor Neufeld's opening remarks are on pages 30–59 of the Court Proceedings.

The words of witnesses for the prosecution, both examination and cross-examination, are recorded on pages 61–452 (interspersed with some other comments by Justice Noble, Prosecutor Neufeld and Defence Lawyer Mark Brayford.

The Supreme Court case quoted in regard to the defence of necessity, *Perka v. the Queen*, is at [1984] 2 S.C.R. 232.

Mark Brayford's opening address to the jury is on pages 453–459 of the Court Proceedings. The defence witnesses, examination, and cross-examination are covered in pages 469–652 of the Court Proceedings.

The interaction between Justice Noble, Prosecutor Neufeld, and Defence Lawyer Brayford regarding the defence of necessity is on pages 655–669 of the Court Proceedings. After the closing statements by the defence (pages 672–707) and the prosecution (pages 707–727), Justice Noble takes away the defence of necessity in his charge to the jury on pages 743–745, as part of his closing charge to the jury on pages 728–772.

Information about the reading of the verdict and Latimer's response can be found in the Canadian Encyclopedia at: encyclopediecanadienne.ca/index.cfm?PgNm=TCE&Params=M1ARTM0011437

Laura's scream of "No! No, no, no!" is recorded in the Court Proceedings as coming from an "unknown female" (page 796).

The questions from the jury and subsequent commentaries regarding sentencing are on pages 777–795 of the Court Proceedings. Subsequent defence counsel submission on sentencing is on pages 811–845. Crown Counsel submission is on pages 846–876. Justice Noble's response, granting a constitutional exemption of the mandatory ten-year minimum, is on robertlatimer.net under court transcripts, or at 1994 N0. 37 J.C.B.

The final ruling of the Supreme Court came on January 18, 2001. See 2001 S.C.R. 3.

CHAPTER 4

My recounting of the Evelyn Martens trial is in *Humanist in Canada*, Issue 152, Spring 2005 (magazine later renamed *Humanist Perspectives*). A later story about her questionable treatment by the CBC appeared in *Humanist Perspectives*, Issue 161, summer 2007.

Information about Lawrence MacAulay, and his edict that the first two years of all murder sentences must be spent in high-security prison, came from discussions and interviews with Robert Latimer, as did information about how long he actually spent in such a prison.

Latimer's letters to the Supreme Court and to various politicians about his belief that his defence was compromised by the notion that a "more effective pain medication" was available for Tracy are all included in his compilation entitled "My Attempts to Understand the Supreme Court's January 18/2001 Decision." My version of this is dated September 2005. A current version can be found at robertlatimer.net.

The testimony of Dr. Robin Menzies regarding Latimer's character are in the Court Proceedings, page 640.

My quote regarding compassion is from an article entitled "Robert Latimer and the Sanctity of Compassion" in *Humanist Perspectives*, Issue 158, Autumn 2008. The article was in response to Latimer's critics who claim that human life ought to be sanctified above all else. I wrote "It is not mere human existence we should hold so sacred—it is human compassion. It is the willingness to help others, especially the most helpless among us, and the willingness to do so even at great personal cost, that we should accord the highest honour. And by that reckoning Robert Latimer is a hero, not a murderer."

CHAPTER 5

My comments about the Parole Board come from public information provided by the National Parole Board, from conversations with Patrick Storey of the NPB Pacific Region (who did not in any way suggest or support my critical comments about the Board) and from a conversation with a former Justice Department employee.

Our inability to assess a person's nature through an interview or simple observation has often been noted. *The Globe and Mail*, Saturday May 27,

2006, in an article entitled "The psychopath in the corner office" said that "Corporate psychopaths are greedy, selfish, deceptive, unreliable and prone to fits of rage. They are also charming and confident, give perfect interviews and quickly become everyone's favourite employee." Were Robert Latimer a psychopath he'd likely have breezed through his parole hearing. See also, for example, Paul Ekman, *Social Research*, Fall 1996, in an article entitled "Why don't we catch liars?"

My observations of the hearing are based on notes I took during the hearing, checked against a recording of the hearing provided by the National Parole Board, through a request supported by Robert Latimer.

CHAPTER 6

The figures for successful appeals came from conversation with Patrick Storey of the NPB's Pacific regional office. The numbers are roughly confirmed by the statistics posted on the National Parole Board's website. For the year 2008–2009 there were 689 appeals, with over 97 per cent of the original Board decisions confirmed.

The full text of Jason Gratl's appeal on behalf of Latimer, as well as the information on the appeal decision, is available at: bccla.org/othercontent/08NPBLatimer.pdf

CHAPTER 7

Information about clemency and pardons is on the website of the National Parole Board: npb-cnlc.gc.ca

The Supreme Court Statement regarding possible clemency for Latimer is in its ruling on the Latimer case, 2001 S.C.R. 3.

There is another pardon process, applied to former convicts who have been out of prison for some time and have demonstrated lawful behaviour during that time. This clears records so that people who once committed a crime, and paid for it, are not punished in a continuing way by having a criminal record. Perhaps one day Latimer will get that pardon, although he would first have to be convinced to apply for it.

CHAPTER 8

The information about how Robert and Laura worked with their children and their school to help protect the children from adverse effects of publicity came from a discussion with Robert's half-sister, Marj Mosienko.

Regarding the misleading suggestion that Laura was going to testify against her husband, see for example Mark Pickup's statement that "although Laura was originally listed as a witness for the prosecution, she switched sides to the defence" at: humanlifematters.org/2008_03_01_archive.html

Laura's comment about "the stupid farm" is reported at: encyclopedie-canadienne.ca/index.cfm?PgNm=TCE&Params=M1ARTM0011437

Laura's comments about the maximum-security prison are at: cbc.ca/canada/story/2001/03/02/latimer_time010302.html

Comments from the CBC interview with Laura can be found in points 31 and 32 at: sfu.ca/~wchane/sa304articles/Klinkhammer.pdf

A report on the candlelight vigil can be found at: cbc.ca/canada/story/2001/03/15/latimer_vigil010315.html

Laura's comments following the denial of day parole are at: ehealthforum.com/health/topic118173.html

Laura's comments following her husband's release are at: canada.com/theprovince/news/story.html?id=a29fbe93-b6ef-451e-bf0e-275ec525ce6c

Regarding the suggestion that Latimer was an "alpha male" see, for example, point 35 at: sfu.ca/~wchane/sa304articles/Klinkhammer.pdf

Laura's comment that her husband was 100 per cent honest is in her testimony; see Court Proceedings, page 514.

For an example of a challenge to the claim of Latimer's honesty see: humanlifematters.org/2008/03/canadas-folk-hero-robert-latimer.html

CHAPTER 9
Some sources for hostile critics of Latimer are as follows:
- normemma.com/artaleof.htm
- cmaj.ca/cgi/content/full/178/3/360
- macleans.ca/canada/national/article.jsp?content=20080306_108153_108153
- chninternational.com/tracybod.htm
- dawn.thot.net/text/t-Tracy_Latimer.html
- ccdenligne.ca/en/humanrights/endoflife/latimer/1997/02a
- suite101.com/article.cfm/special_needs/43639

- lifesitenews.com/ldn/2002/jan/020117a.html
- arpacanada.ca/index.php/issuesresearch/
  pro-life/81-latimers-appeal-for-the-royal-prerogative-of-mercy
- theinterim.com/2002/feb/01latimer.html

There are many attempts to explain the seemingly contradictory position of religious conservatives that euthanasia and abortion disrespect human life but that capital punishment and war do not. In a recent statement on this topic the Catholic Archbishop of Denver Charles Chaput wrote that "the death penalty is not intrinsically evil (like abortion and euthanasia are)." He further wrote that "these different issues—euthanasia, the death penalty, war, genocide and abortion—do not all have the same gravity or moral content." But do they all not disrespect the sanctity of human life— take the ending of life out of God's hands? And is euthanasia, in the case where a person wants to die, more evil than killing an enemy soldier, who wants to live? There is of course much more to be said on this topic.

The statement from Pope Benedict XVI in October, 2008 reaffirmed the Church's opposition to birth control. See: theinterim.com/2002/feb/01latimer.html

I was able to watch the entire Supreme Court hearing on DVDs loaned to me by Robert Latimer. The Court ruling is at 2001 S.C.R. 3.

CHAPTER 10

See the excellent book *Jury Nullification: The Evolution of a Doctrine*, by Clay S. Conrad, Carolina Academic Press, 1998. Also see:

- isil.org/resources/lit/history-jury-null.html
- fija.org
- law.umkc.edu/faculty/projects/ftrials/zenger/nullification.html

The statement of Justice Chrumka is quoted in the Supreme Court judgment on the case at 2006 SCC 47. The initial appeal judgment by the Alberta Court of Appeal is at 2005 ABCA 202. See also:

- thecourt.ca/2007/01/23/r-v-krieger-jury-nullification-and-the-limits-of-descriptive-mens-rea/
- smhilaw.com/Publications/ART-0507-JuryNullification.pdf

The Supreme Court ruling that in effect legalized abortion, and which in effect banned future defences based upon jury nullification, is at [1988] 1 S.C.R. 30. Chief Justice Dickson's statement on jury nullification is on pages 77-79.

Justice Noble's discussion with the jury about sentencing in the Latimer case was discussed briefly in Chapter 3, and the sources are cited in the notes for that chapter.

The final Supreme Court ruling on Latimer, January 18, 2001, is at 2001 S.C.R. 3.

Obama's comments were made in a White House Press Conference on May 1, 2009.

CHAPTER 11

Latimer's comments following his conviction, and the comments by a juror, are reported at: encyclopediecanadienne.ca/index.cfm?PgNm=TCE& Params=M1ARTM0011437

The Sue Rodriguez case has been extensively reported on. A detailed government review of the case is given at: dsp-psd.pwgsc.gc.ca/Collection-R/ LoPBdP/BP/bp349-e.htm

Information on Oregon's *Death with Dignity Act* can be found at: oregon. gov/DHS/ph/pas/

Information on Washington State's *Death with Dignity Act* can be found at: doh.wa.gov/dwda/

Montana's Supreme Court, on December 31, 2009, ruled that physician-assisted suicide is legal. See: ama-assn.org/amednews/2010/01/18/ prsb0118.htm

A compilation of information about assisted suicide and euthanasia in various parts of the world has been compiled by Derek Humphrey, at: assistedsuicide.org/suicide_laws.html

For a news report on Britain's new approach to prosecuting assisted suicide see: cbc.ca/world/story/2010/02/25/uk-assisted-suicide.html

The Senate Report, *Of Life and Death*, can be found at: parl.gc.ca/35/1/ parlbus/commbus/senate/Com-e/euth-e/rep-e/lad-e.htm

The Angus Reid poll of February 2010 is at: visioncritical. com/?s=euthanasia

PHOTOGRAPHIC
CREDITS

INDEX

2